To the books I read as a child, which got me into this. And to the people who put up with me, now that I've gotten into this.
– K.S.

HELVETIQ publishing has been supported by the Swiss Federal Office of Culture with a structural grant for the years 2021–2025.

Made possible by the support of:

Govern de les Illes Balears – Conselleria de Turisme, Cultura i Esports | institut d'estudis baleàrics | institut ramon llull

Big Digs
Amazing Underground Constructions

Originally published by Editorial Juventud as:
Túneles
Construcciones increíbles de aquí y de allá

Foreign Rights: Tormenta
www.tormentalibros.com

Translation from Spanish: Marc Correa
Cover design, typesetting and layout (English edition): Ewelina Proczko and Ajša Zdravković

ISBN: 978-3-03964-124-6
Second edition: 2026
Printed in China

Blumenrain 34
4051 Basel
Switzerland

HELVETIQ helvetiq.com

FSC MIX Paper from responsible sources FSC® C167893

KIKO SÁNCHEZ

BIG DIGS

AMAZING UNDERGROUND **CONSTRUCTIONS**

Translated by
Marc Correa

Follow these tunnels and you won't get lost!

BIG DIGS

AMAZING UNDERGROUND **CONSTRUCTIONS**

TUNNEL OF CONTENTS

See you later!

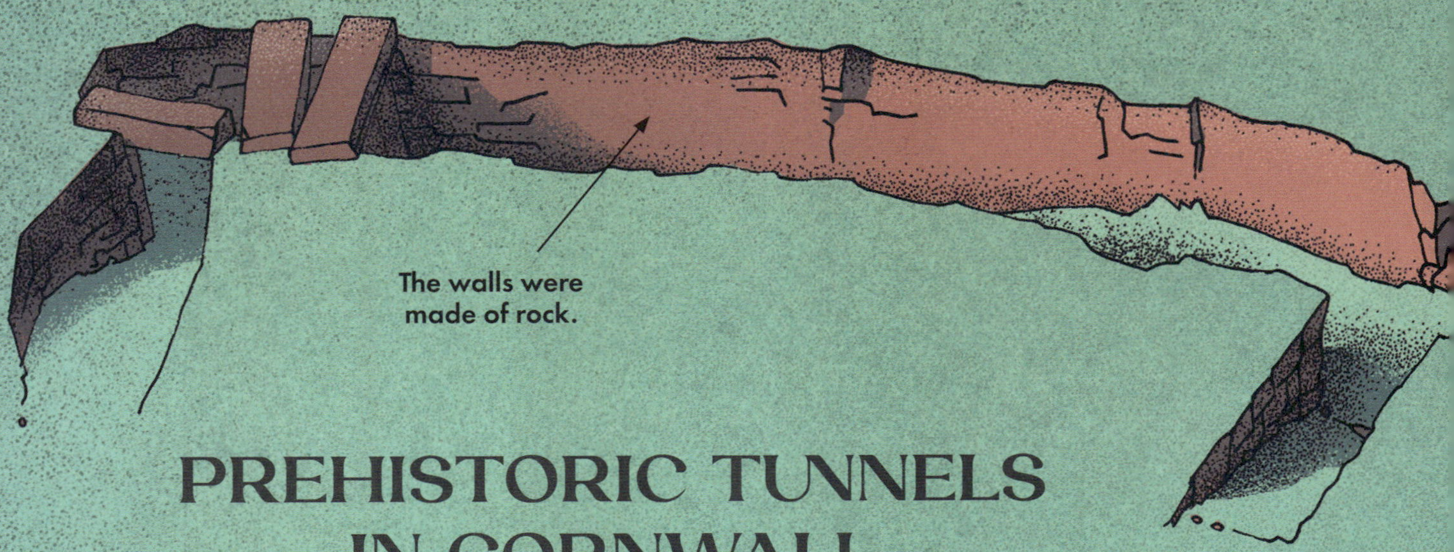

PREHISTORIC TUNNELS IN CORNWALL

(Cornwall, United Kingdom, 1100–300 BCE)

In the old Celtic language called Cornish, *fogou* means a cave or subterranean structure. More than 200 *fogous* have been found in Cornwall, but unlike most caves, *fogous* are not natural: they were dug into the ground and then covered to simulate tunnels.

Haliggye Fogou is the most famous one. It is very well preserved, but over the years it has been pillaged by collectors and nosy people, and there is very little of it left that we can use to learn about the past.

The antechambers lead to two long tunnels that are barely 2.5 feet (75 cm) tall at their lowest points. The only way to move inside the tunnels is by crouching, but at one point they get so dark and narrow you can't go any further!

HOW WERE THEY BUILT?

To build these tunnels they had to dig underground to the right depth. Then, they paved the trench and formed the ceiling with huge slabs. Afterwards they covered the whole thing with soil.

The slabs were brought from quarries far away. We don't know how they did it, but our best guess is that they dragged them on sleds. That's some hard work!

WHAT WERE THEY USED FOR?

The tunnels had narrow walls and low ceilings, and their entrances were easily spotted, so it's unlikely people used them as homes or hideouts. Some people think they might have been sacred burial sites. Others think they were used to store grain, but the humidity inside the fogous would have ruined any food.
What do you think?

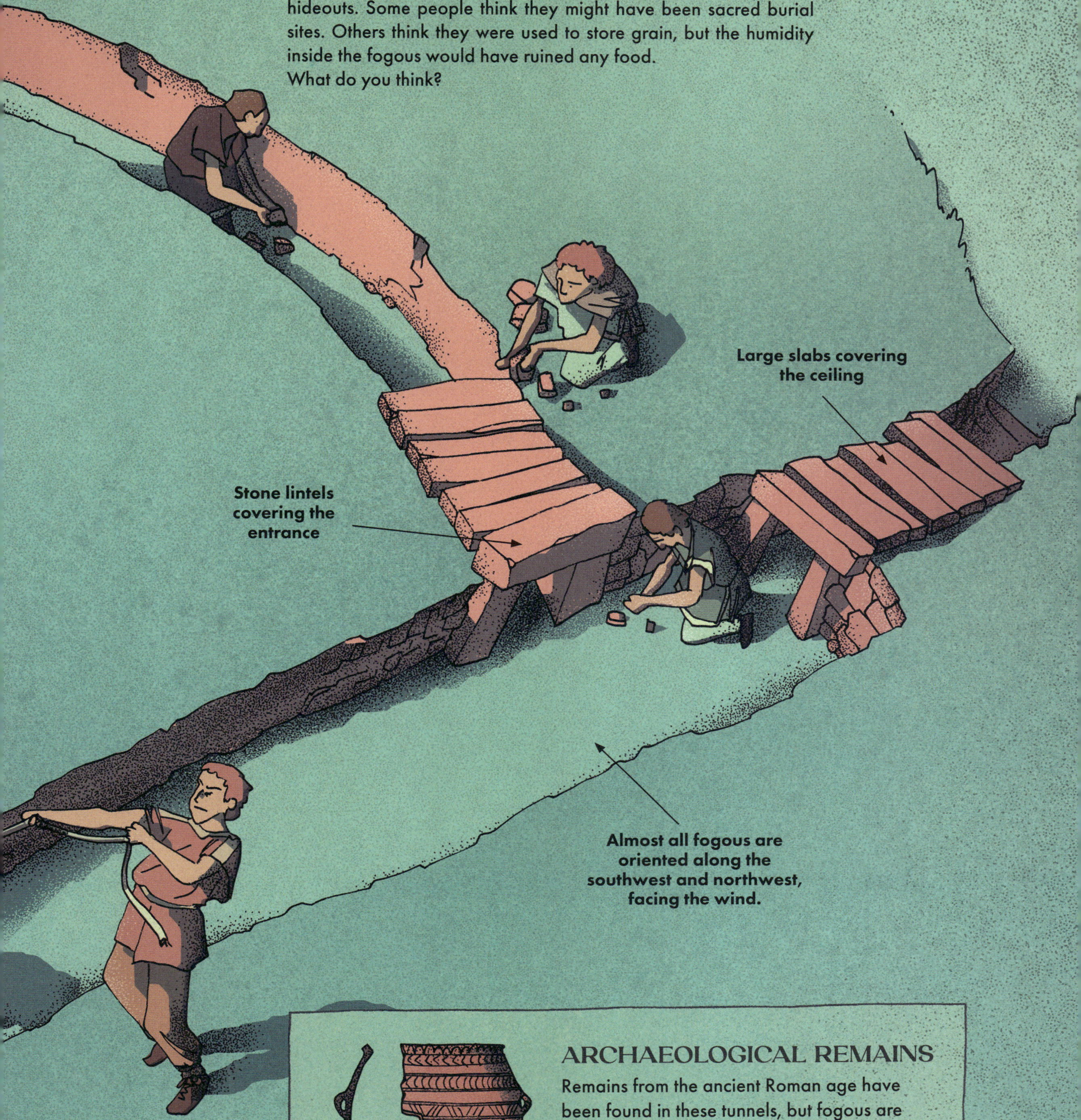

ARCHAEOLOGICAL REMAINS

Remains from the ancient Roman age have been found in these tunnels, but fogous are actually much older than the Roman Empire. Maybe a group of Romans threw a party in the old tunnel?

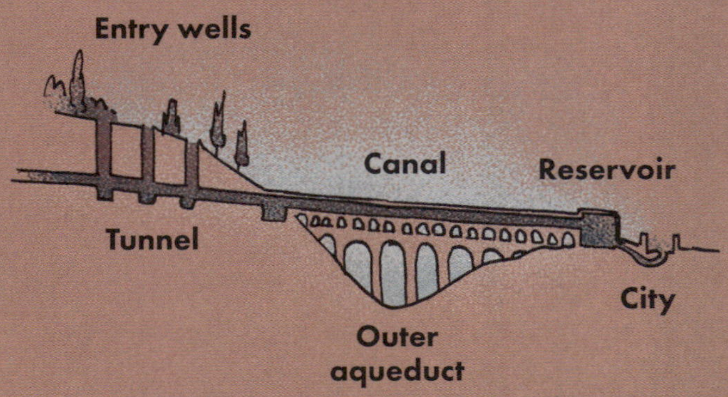

The Romans used aqueducts to transport water across great distances. They built bridges on stone arches over rivers, with a narrow water canal on top. The canal was covered to keep sunlight, dust and bird poop out of the water. These aqueducts are built so well that many of them are still standing today and could be used again.

THE GADARA AQUEDUCT

(Modern day Jordan, between 1st and 2nd centuries)

If this structure doesn't seem impressive enough, how about this: it was built almost 2000 years ago! Gadara was located on a trade route to India and China, so the Romans were very interested in it. Since it's a dry area, they had to reroute a river and build an aqueduct 105 miles (170 km) long, which ran underground for about 60 miles (100 km). It supplied water to ten cities.

It took the Romans almost a century to finish it. If you tried to do this all by yourself you would cover maybe 4 inches (10 cm) a day. It would take you more than 2000 years to finish the tunnel!

BATHS AND FOUNTAINS

The Romans really loved their water, and they had hundreds of fountains and bath houses in their cities. They used up to 130 gallons (500 liters) of water a day per person!

HOW DID THEY DO IT?

Ancient Romans didn't have compasses, but they had ways to find their bearings inside the mountain using weights and string.

First, they built a staircase from the surface and used lengths of string to measure the depth. Then, the workers dug a tunnel up to the next section. Little by little they made the tunnel bigger until it reached the size they wanted. When the tunnel had the right dimensions, they sealed it with cement to make it waterproof.

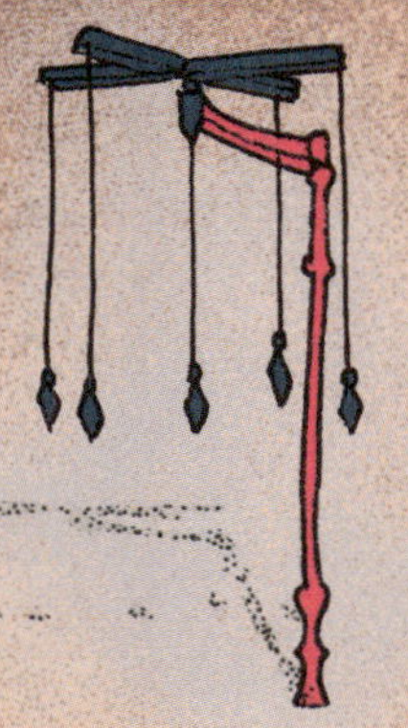

The tunnel was designed to have a slope of about one foot per mile. Only a little more than that, and the water would flow at more than 185 gallons (700 liters) per second, and the tunnel would collapse.

TEMPLE OF THE FEATHERED SERPENT

(Teotihuacan, modern day Mexico, 3rd century)

One of the most mysterious tunnels in America was discovered by accident. In 2003, heavy rain had been falling on the ancient complex of Teotihuacan, in Mexico. Archaeologist Sergio Gómez Chávez was working in one of the temples and noticed that erosion caused by the water had carved a small hole near a sacrificial altar.

Hoping to find how that happened, he grabbed a flashlight and some ropes and descended 46 feet (14 m) into the hole. He found that some heavy boulders were blocking the entrance to an unknown tunnel. How about that?

Gómez was the first human to set foot there in 1700 years. After that, a team of archaeologists spent eight years clearing the tunnel. If that sounds like a long time, it's because they didn't want to damage anything and only used simple tools. The tunnel turned out to be about 330 feet (100 m) long, and it reached deep into the Pyramid of Quetzalcoatl.

WHERE MEN BECOME GODS

Important rituals took place in this tunnel. Through it, a new leader would descend to the underworld, where they would be granted divine power. They would then emerge from the depths crowned as a god. Teotihuacan literally means "where men become gods."

THE CITADEL

Teotihuacan had the largest population of all Mesoamerican cities. Its citadel, located at the heart of the city, was so big that all the inhabitants of the city could fit there together!

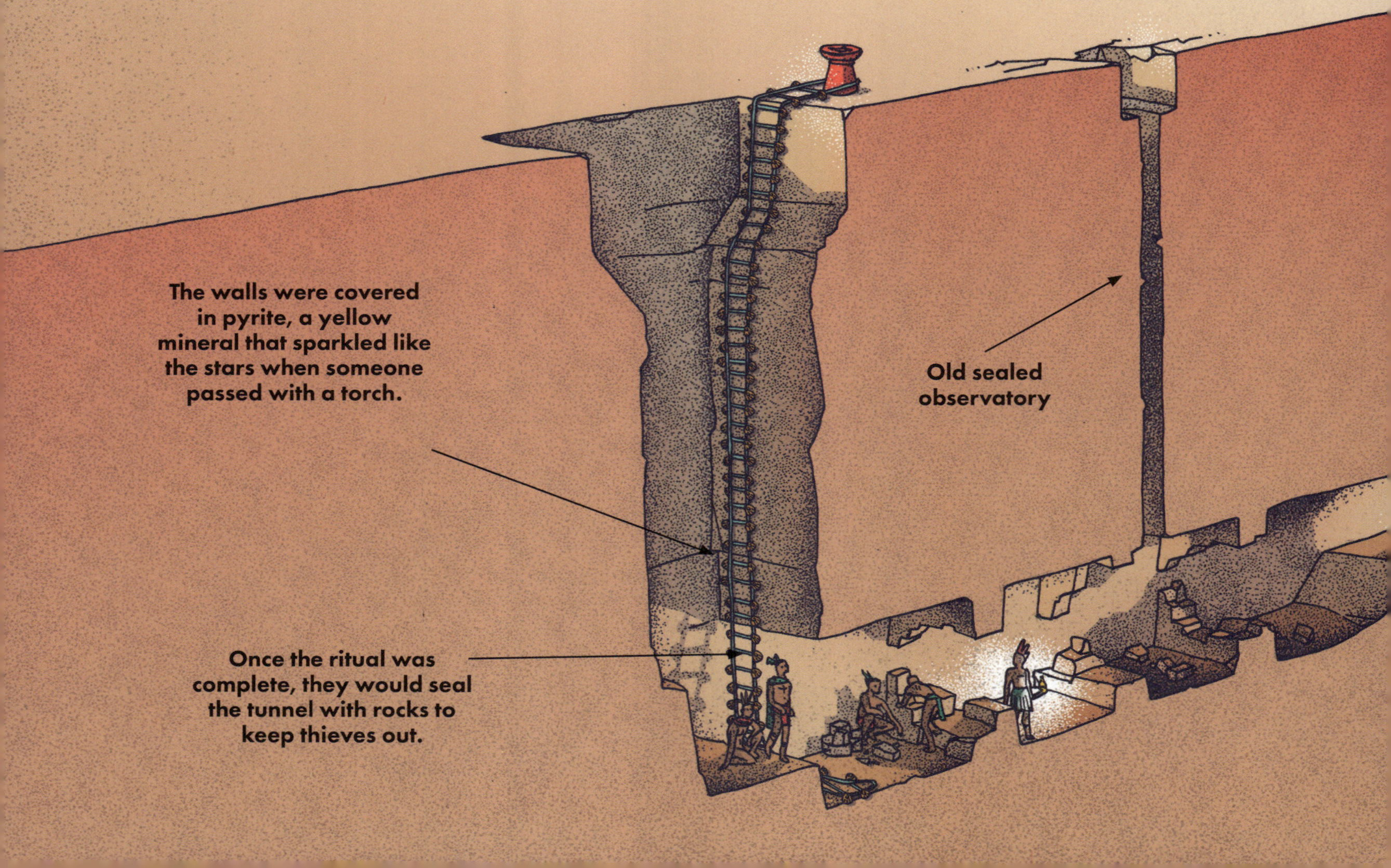

TIMBER!

The ancient Mesoamerican civilizations used very advanced techniques when they built their pyramids, because these were expected to survive regular earthquakes. The Mexica people liked to use adobe, stone and something called Teotihuacan cement for the pyramids; but to build the rest of the city, wood was good enough.

They used wood for cooking and heating up their homes, too. They used so much wood that they exhausted the resources of their forests. This is one of the main reasons they abandoned the city.

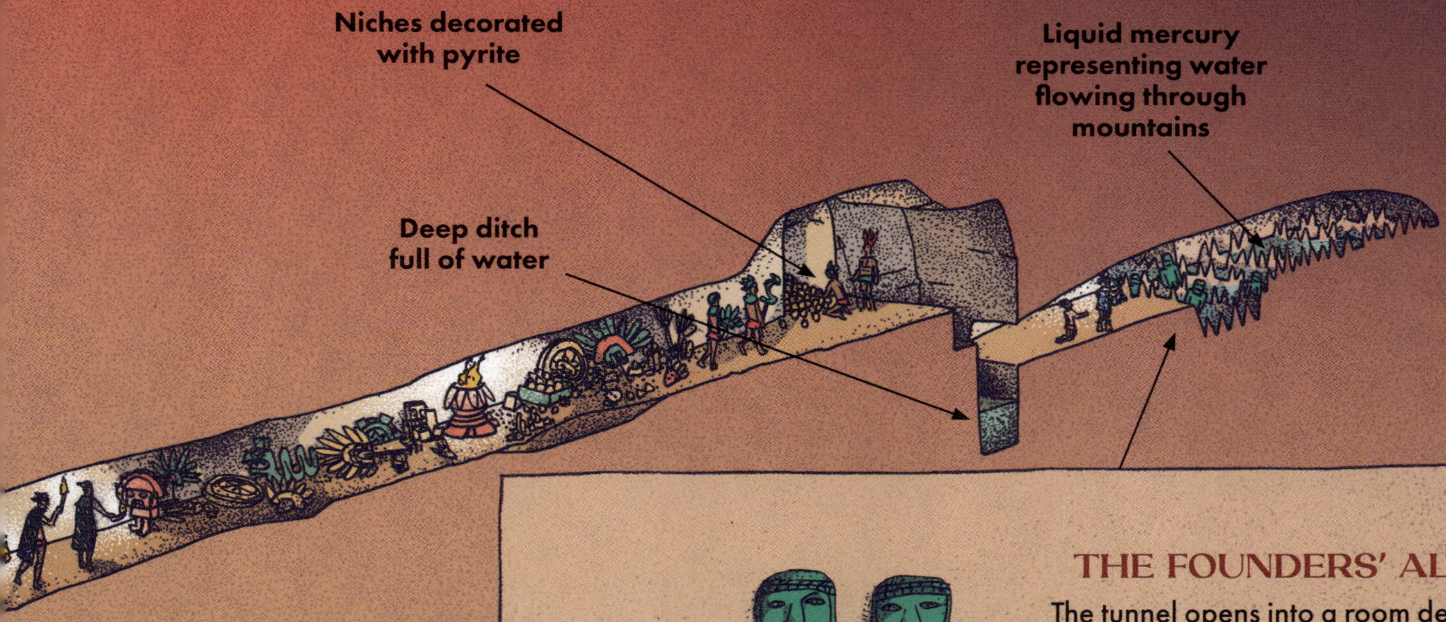

THE FOUNDERS' ALTAR

The tunnel opens into a room decorated with sculptures of the men and women who founded the city. The women are bigger, because women were more important than men in their society.

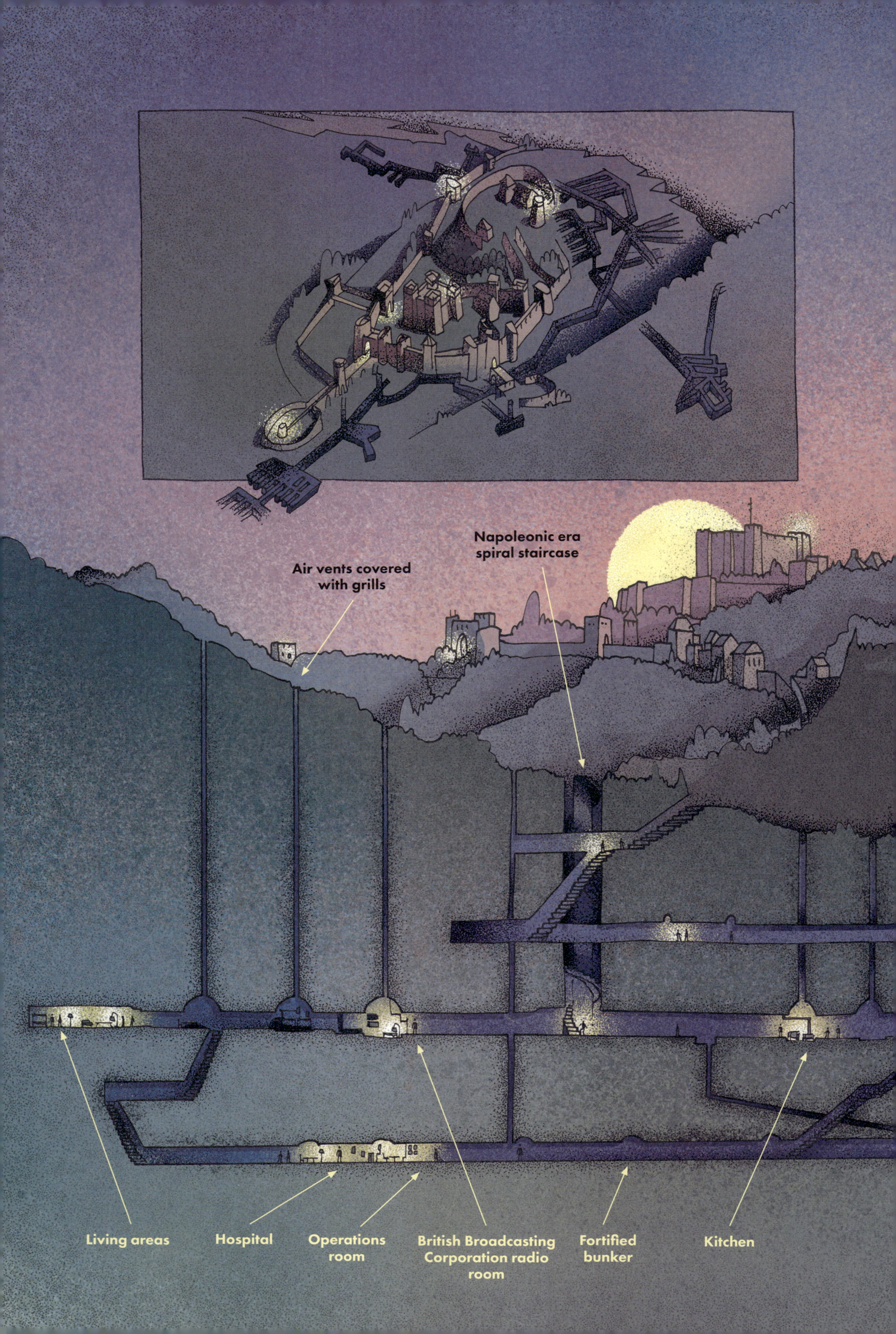
Air vents covered with grills
Napoleonic era spiral staircase
Living areas
Hospital
Operations room
British Broadcasting Corporation radio room
Fortified bunker
Kitchen

TUNNELS UNDER DOVER CASTLE

(Dover, United Kingdom, 12th century)

Dover Castle was built on a cliff and had walls so tall it could repel any attack. This was useful in times of war, but it had a drawback: the castle could be besieged. In the Middle Ages, if you couldn't take the enemy fortress, you had to block all supply routes going into it. Sooner or later, the enemy would have to surrender, because everyone needs food and water.

To counter that, the people of Dover had an idea. They built tunnels that allowed them to get in and out of the castle undetected, so they could survive a siege for months. The tunnel network was expanded during the Napoleonic Wars of the 19th century. We still haven't found all the tunnels they built!

In 1940, Prime Minister Churchill visited the area and saw that Nazi warships were sailing too close to the coast. After World War Two, sieges were a thing of the past, but now people in Europe were scared of a nuclear threat. Churchill decided to expand the tunnel network and build a vast shelter into it. The bunker was fortified to keep the soldiers stationed inside safe, and so it could be used as emergency government headquarters. It even had its own hospital.

After the Berlin Wall fell and the nuclear threat diminished, the tunnels were abandoned. Some of them were later opened to the public, and you can find messages carved in the walls. You can even find stuff left behind by the soldiers before they went home!

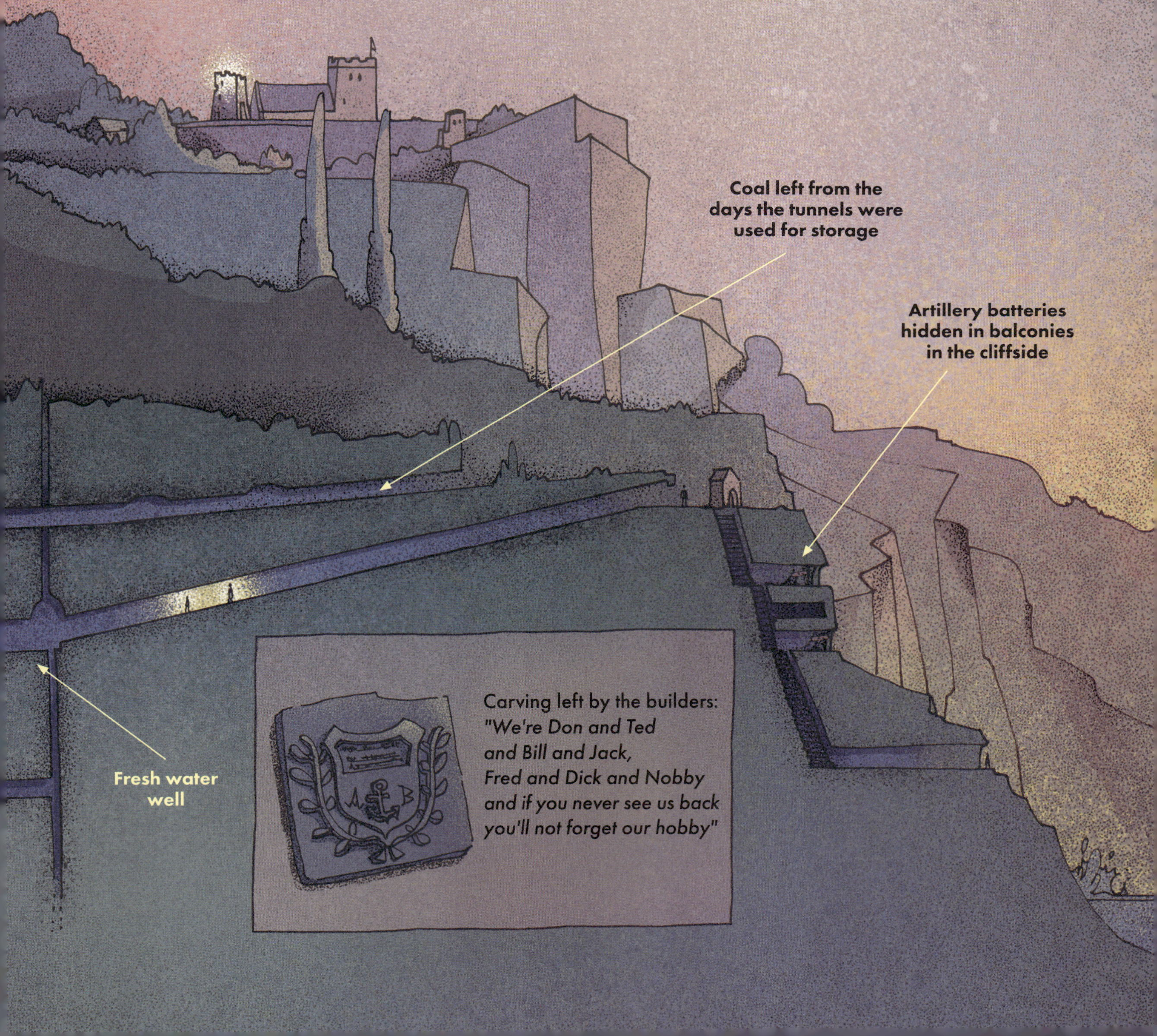

QUINTA DA REGALEIRA

(Sintra, Portugal, 1902–1912)

The first thing you'll see when you climb up the twisting path to Quinta da Regaleira is a huge grey manor surrounded by a dense forest, crowned by large pinnacles and decorated with enigmatic statues. But the real mystery lies in the gardens and in the tunnels inside the mountain.

In the early 20th century, a Brazilian millionaire called Carvalho Monteiro hired an architect to build a palace in Sintra. Monteiro was a Freemason and he wanted his philosophy to show in his new home. The Freemasons need special places to gather because they are forbidden from revealing their secrets to outsiders. These places are hidden and full of mysteries, and even today we still don't really know everything about what they did in the Quinta.

Want to find out?

THE INITIATION WELL

A secret stairwell hidden in the forest represents the journey from darkness into the light. It's guarded by two statues shaped like lionfish. Water runs down the stairs and the nine levels of the well, which represent the nine circles of Hell. People who wanted to join the order had to climb down the stairs as part of the initiation ritual. A secret entrance at the bottom leads to a series of tunnels connecting various places in the gardens and the palace. Watch out for bats!

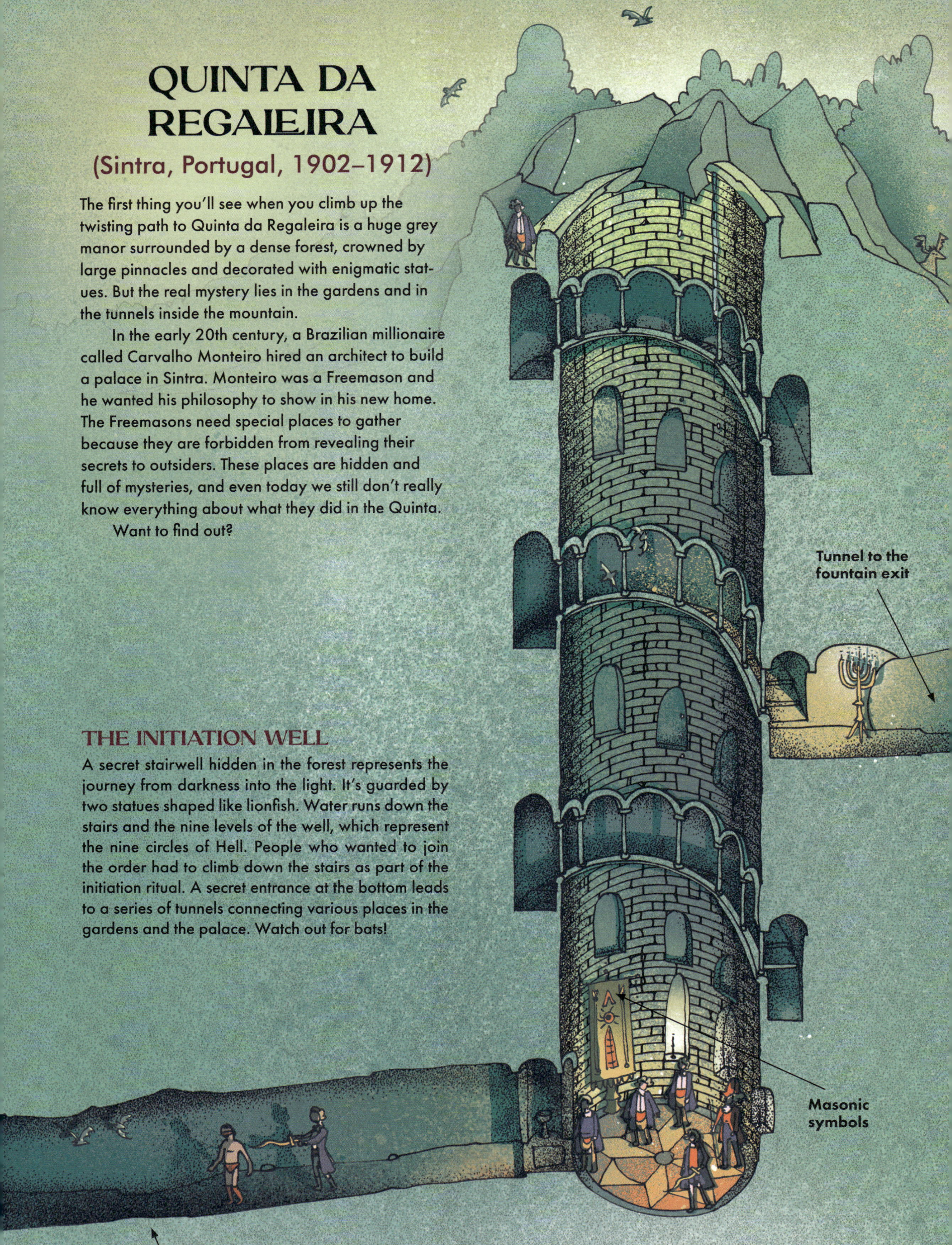

The manor has an alchemy lab meant for research on the philosopher's stone. This substance was believed to grant anyone infinite riches and eternal youth.

THE FOREST

The garden leads to neat paths that go into the trees. But as you go deeper into the forest it becomes wild and messy, like an unexplored jungle.

WHAT'S THAT NOISE?

Those who walk by this tower will hear a loud rumble that sounds like a storm, even when it's sunny. Beneath the tower, a huge water reservoir feeds the fountains in the garden.

CONSEQUENCES

Dams and reservoirs had to be built to establish the water system. This changed the natural course of the river, which caused catastrophic floods. It's hard to predict how projects like this will impact the environment.

BYPASS

In 2013 the tunnel was split into several canals. That way some sections could be closed for repairs. This work turned out to be so complex that it's still not finished.

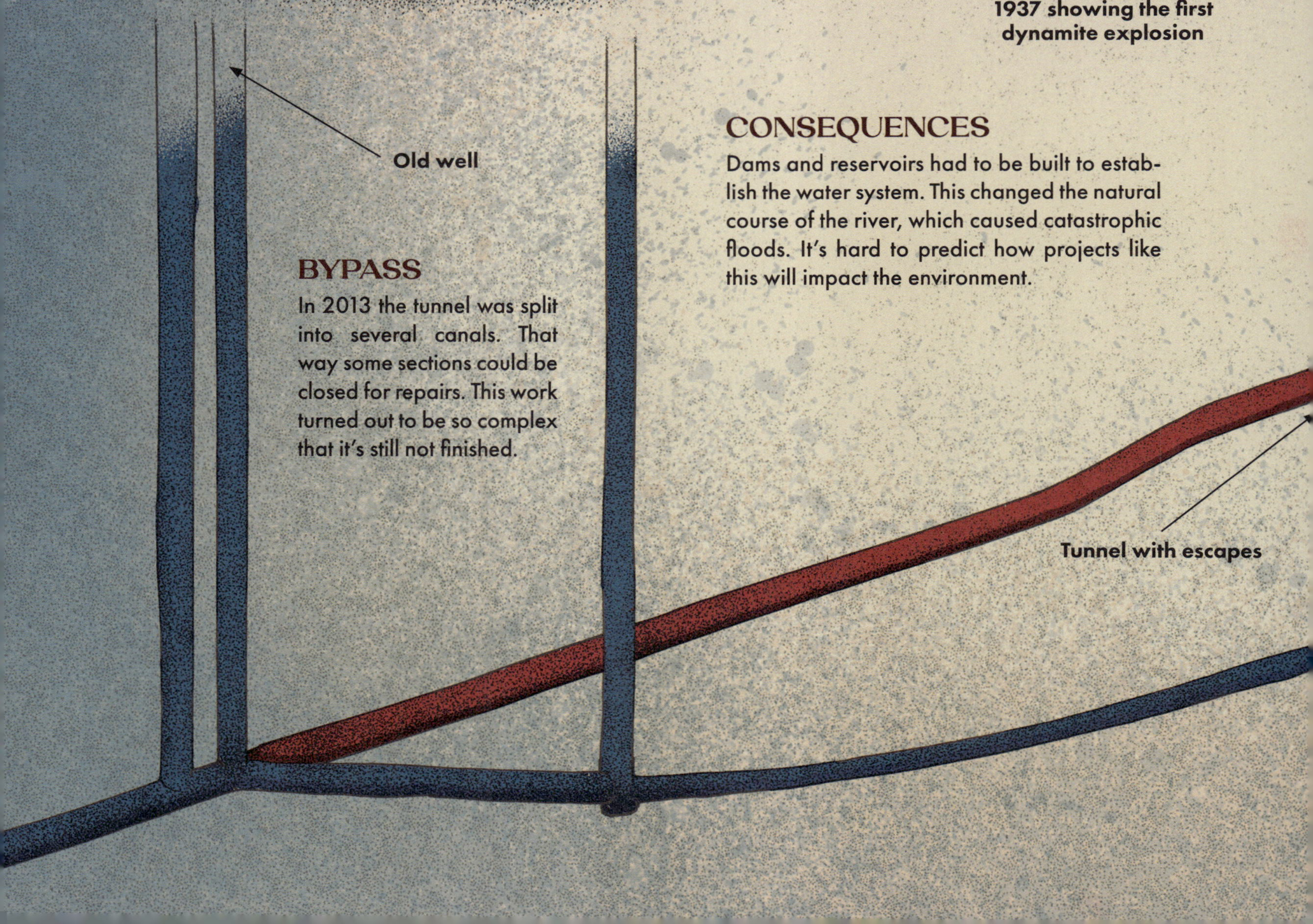

THE DELAWARE AQUEDUCT

(New York State, United States, 1937–1944)

The people who settled down in what we call New York used simple wells, but eventually these ran out or became contaminated. Where could they get fresh water without underground reserves? From rivers and lakes, of course. In the 18th century they began building aqueducts to bring water from several reservoirs.

During the 20th century, New York grew into the most populous city in the United States. It became a very thirsty city, and soon they needed a bigger aqueduct. In 1939 work on the impressive Delaware Aqueduct began, and the plan was to bring about 1.3 billion gallons of water from a river 100 miles (160 km) away from the city. And that's only half of what the city needed!

The tunnel had to be built fast and cheap, since the country was busy with the Second World War. The method chosen was demolition: they blew up the bedrock with dynamite, then they built the tunnel with arches and covered it with concrete. But the tunnel is so long that even with such a simple method it wasn't finished until 1965.

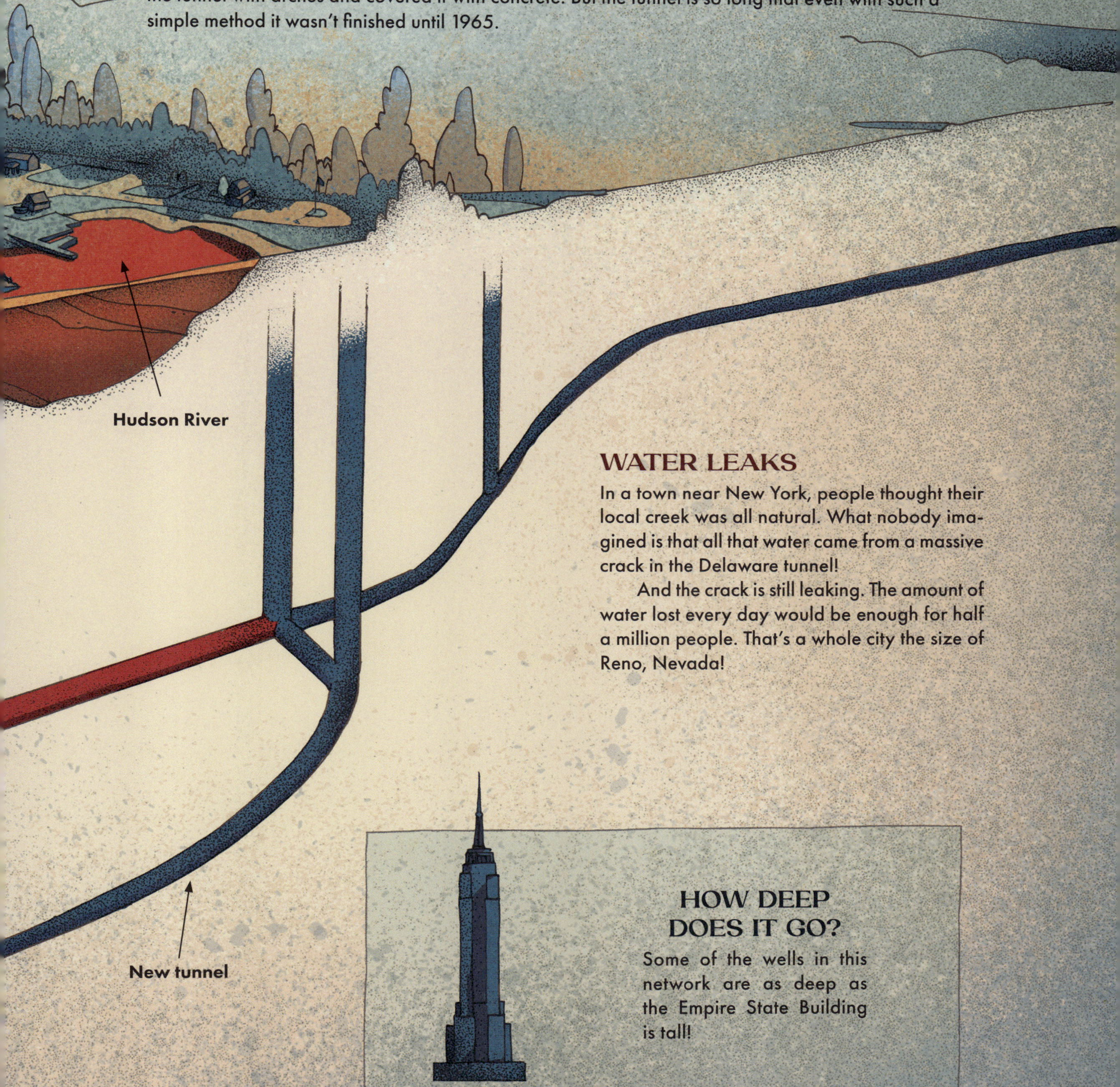

WATER LEAKS

In a town near New York, people thought their local creek was all natural. What nobody imagined is that all that water came from a massive crack in the Delaware tunnel!

And the crack is still leaking. The amount of water lost every day would be enough for half a million people. That's a whole city the size of Reno, Nevada!

HOW DEEP DOES IT GO?

Some of the wells in this network are as deep as the Empire State Building is tall!

A BLUNDER ON LIVE TV

The fall of the Wall was unexpected. On November 9th, 1989, the government decided to open the wall the following day to let a few people through. But on a live press conference, the government spokesperson suggested the wall was open to everyone.

That night thousands of people rushed the border and began to cross over. The guards didn't know what was going on, but they couldn't stop them. Soon, people began tearing down the wall with their bare hands!

On the other side, friends and family were waiting.

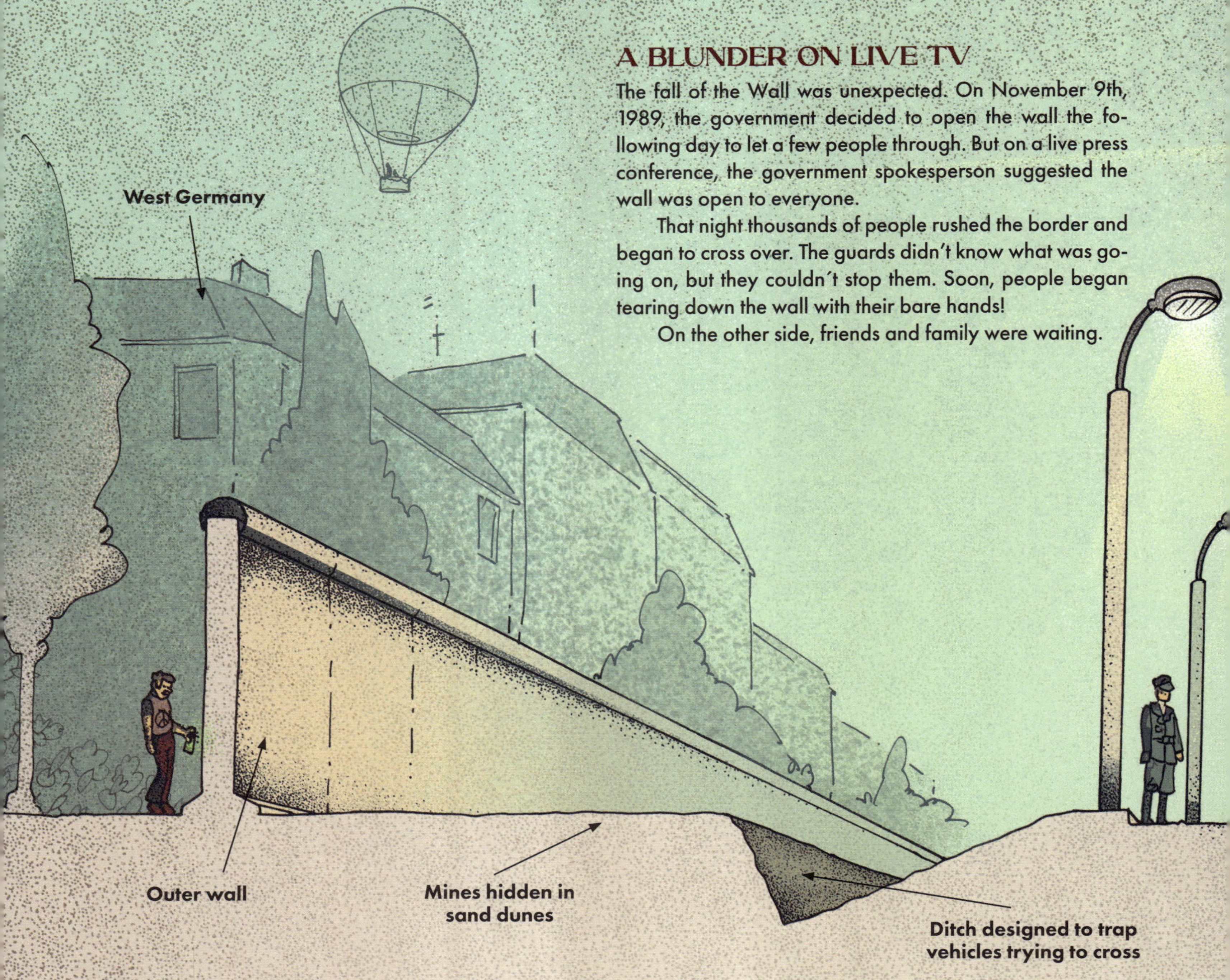

TUNNELS UNDER THE BERLIN WALL

(Berlin, Germany, 1961–1989)

For almost 30 years, Berlin was split by a wall. Going over it was almost impossible because it was over 10 feet (3 m) tall. The area around it was guarded by armed soldiers and guard dogs, and it was equipped with barbed wire, antipersonnel mines, electric fences and machine guns. This area was known as the "death strip." Why did they build this wall across the city?

Germany was split in two halves after World War Two: the capitalist Federal Republic of Germany (FDR), and the German Democratic Republic (GDR), which was an extension of the Soviet Union. Berlin was caught in the middle, with West Berlin belonging to the FDR, and East Berlin as part of the GDR.

West Berlin was like an island inside the GDR, and that was a big difficulty for the communist authorities. Between 1949 and 1961 more than two and a half million people escaped from the East side over to the West in search of a better life. To stop this, the government built a massive, 100-mile-long wall on August 13th, 1961. They built the whole wall overnight!

Many people tried to escape from East Berlin while it was closed. Some 262 people died while trying to go over the wall, and thousands of others were arrested. Still, many did make it.

More than 5000 Berliners escaped by hiding in cars, crossing through tunnels under the streets, using ziplines between buildings, and even homemade hot air balloons built out of fabric!

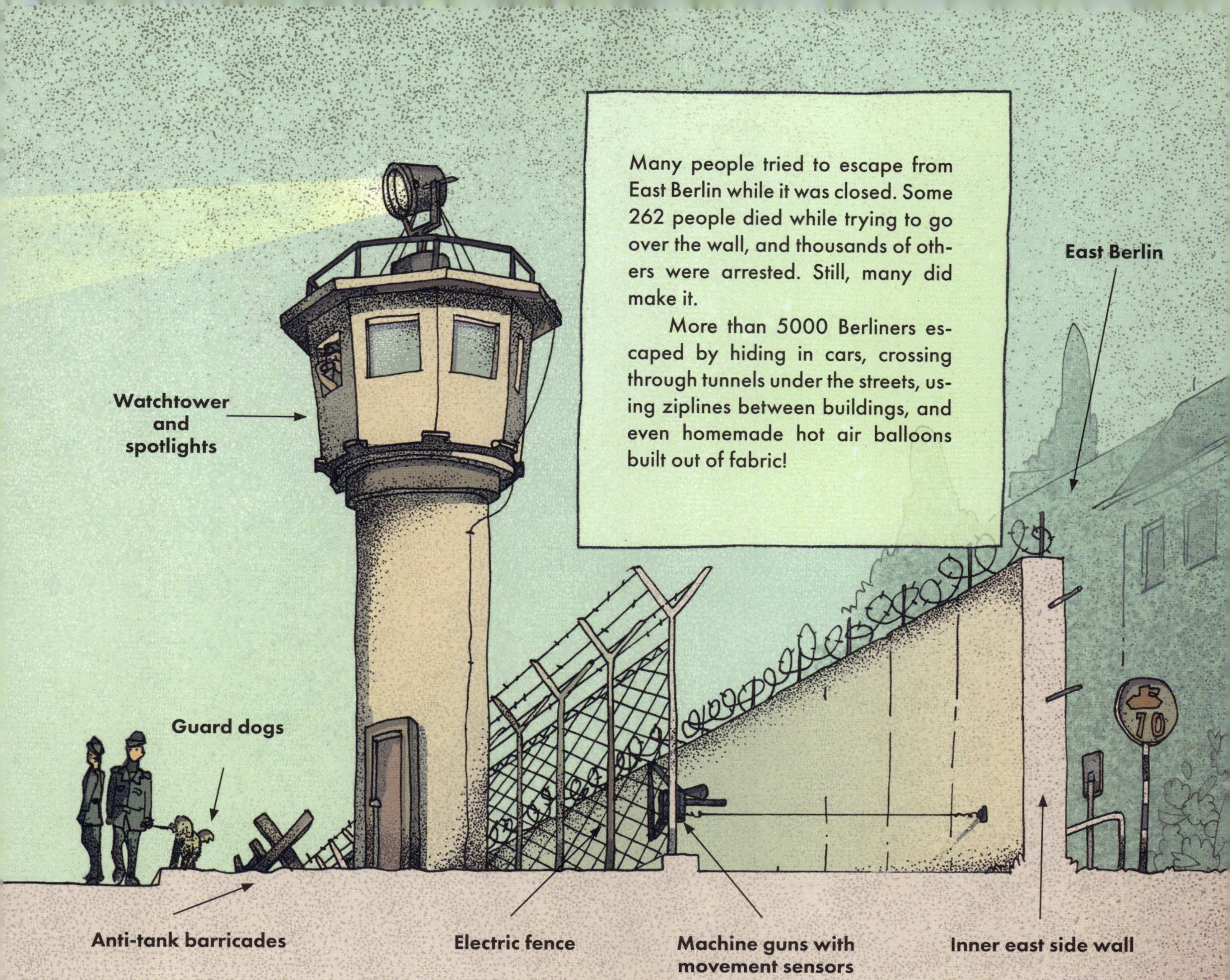

TUNNEL 57

Almost 70 tunnels were dug, and some of them passed right under the watchtowers.
Tunnel 57, named for the number of people that escaped through it, is the most famous one. It was 475 feet (145 m) long and 40 feet (12 m) deep. East Berliners dug the tunnels at night using crude tools like shovels and hammers, and sometimes their bare hands. But this wasn't amateur work: many of the tunnels were designed by expert engineers.

HARD WORK

Mingxin and his buddies didn't have the right tools for the job, and they barely managed to dig three feet deep on the first day. They almost gave up. The tunnel was finished in 1977. Even though it's one of the world's most dangerous roads, lots of tourists want to see it with their own eyes.

DON'T LOOK DOWN!

Before they built the tunnel, the only way to reach Guoliang was by climbing 720 very steep wooden steps on the cliffside. It was so dangerous that many people had never dared leave their town.

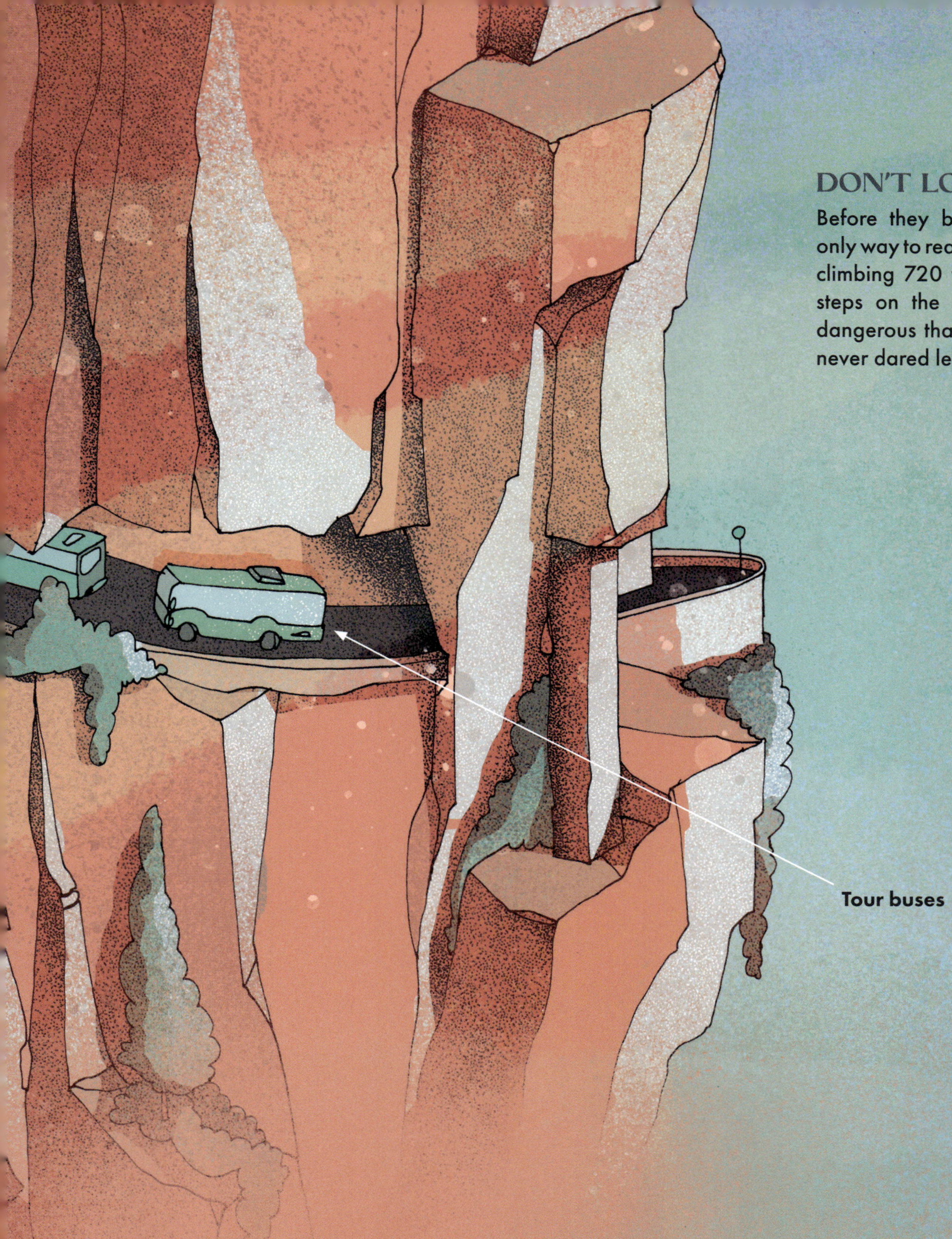

THE GUOLIANG TUNNEL

(Guoliang, China, 1972–1977)

Guoliang is a small mountain town in a remote area of China. To reach it, people had to climb a dangerous stairway carved on a cliffside. The nearest school was at the base of the mountain, so children had to climb up and down the stairs every day. That's how much they loved school!

One day after a huge snowstorm, in 1972, a little girl slipped and fell down the cliff. After this tragedy, a local called Shen Mingxin convinced some of his friends to start digging into the mountain and build a road.

They weren't engineers and they didn't have any training. But with some basic tools and techniques, they slowly carved a tunnel that followed the natural shape of the mountainside. Some parts of the tunnel had windows to the open air, while other parts of the road ran right along the edge. Little by little, this group of 12 people finished this impressive engineering project.

It only took them only five years to dig the tunnel, which is three quarters of a mile (1.2 km) long, 16 feet (5 m) tall and 13 feet (4m) wide. Today, people come from all over the world to see the tunnel and take photos in it. Hard to imagine it was built by only a handful of people, right?

THE KOLA SUPERDEEP BOREHOLE

(Kola peninsula, modern day Russia, 1970–1992)

In Jules Verne's novel *Journey to the Center of the Earth*, the protagonists reach our planet's depths through a natural well. In real life, such a journey is impossible due to the properties of the Earth's crust. But back in 1970, the Russians tried something similar: they dug a vertical tunnel, not to reach the center of the Earth, but to study the structure and composition of its crust.

A 3-mile (5 km) section of the well collapsed when they were 7.5 miles (12 km) deep. Years of work, all buried under the rubble. They decided to start again from 4.3 miles (7 km), and they reached 7.5 miles again by 1983. Nobody had ever drilled that deep! They stopped drilling in 1992, at a depth close to 8 miles (12.8 km), because down there the temperature was almost 600°F (300°C). Plus, the bedrock there was mixed with explosive hydrogen gas. That sure made drilling difficult!

The project was abandoned in 2006 because they ran out of budget.

DISCOVERIES GALORE

In the old days, people who wanted to study the earth's interior had to settle for the stuff that came out of volcanoes. That's why the Russian scientists got excited as their tunnel reached deeper. Among other things, they found plankton fossils in some of the deep crust samples.

THE DRILLING HEAD

They used advanced techniques to dig this tunnel: as the drilling head dug its way into the rock, they injected a special clay into the walls of the well to make it hard and stop it from collapsing.

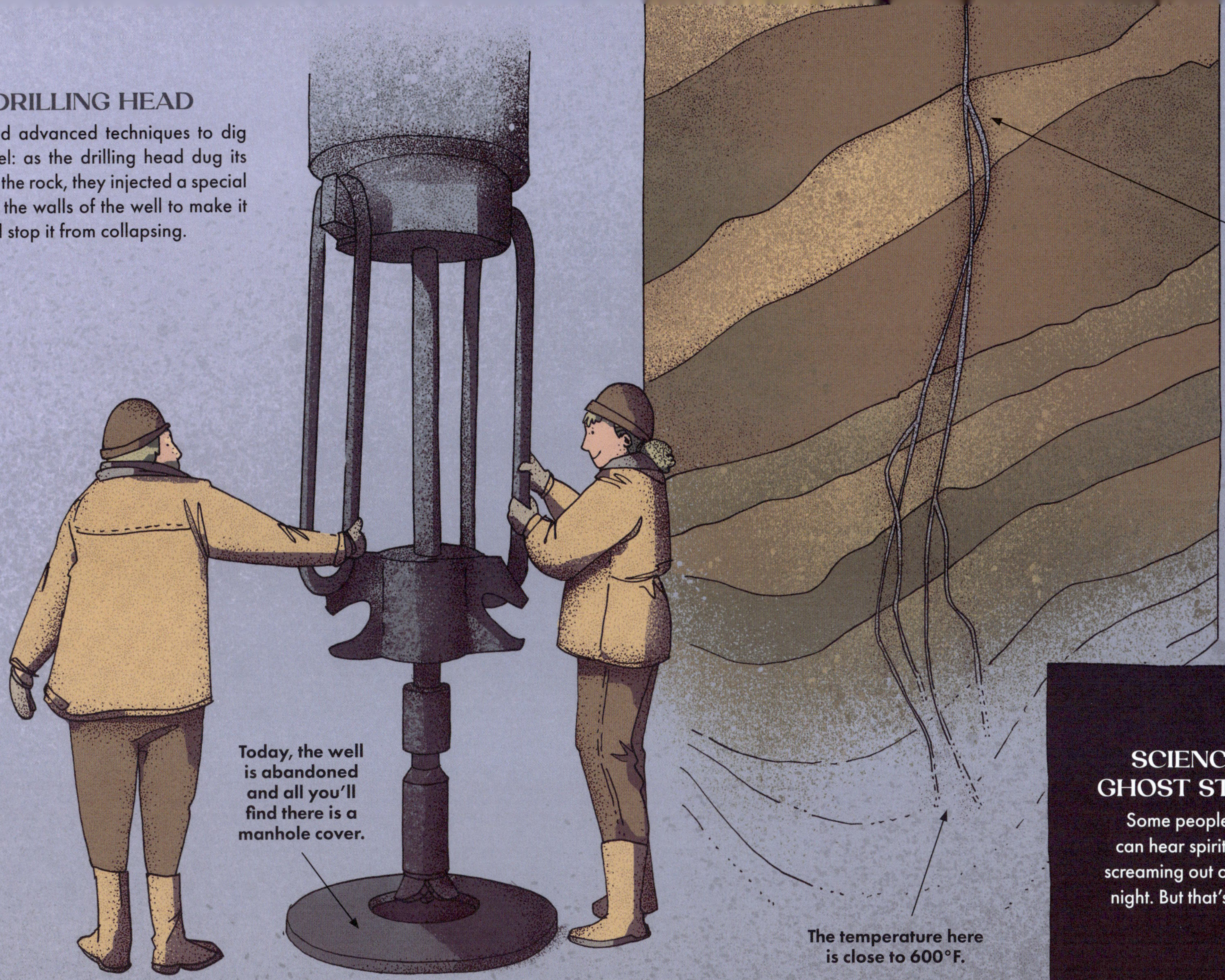

SCIENCE OR GHOST STORIES?

Some people say you can hear spirits from hell screaming out of the well at night. But that's nonsense!

THE AUDACITY!

The police are still finding abandoned tunnels in places you wouldn't imagine. They found one that went from a house in Tijuana to a basement in a fried chicken joint.

The latest discovery is a tunnel with its entrance next to a National Guard station! These tunnels were built close to noisy airports so nobody could hear what was going on inside them.

In addition to drugs and contraband, the Mexican cartels also smuggle people and cash through the tunnels. Almost two hundred tunnels have been found since 2016, but officials believe there are thousands of them still in operation.

NARCO-TUNNELS IN TIJUANA

(Tijuana, Baja California, Mexico – San Diego, Alta California, USA)

Nobody is supposed to cross the US-Mexico border without permission. In some places in Tijuana a wall stops illegal goods like drugs and weapons from entering the country. To go around the sections of wall you'd have to be brave or crazy enough to trek across a vast, dangerous desert. Instead, smugglers went back to basics: they dug tunnels. They weren't going to settle for a small, half-baked tunnel, because millions of dollars were at stake. This operation had to work perfectly, no matter the cost.

The most impressive tunnel found so far is almost one mile (1.5 km) long and is quite sophisticated and well-equipped. The entrance is hidden, and once inside, an elevator takes you down 70 feet (21 m) to a tunnel that's barely tall enough to stand in. It's only 2 feet (60 cm) wide. This tunnel features a lighting system, water drainage, telephone lines, electric rails and wagons, and even air conditioning!

When the police found the tunnel in 2020, they also found a separate offshoot that was still under construction. It was meant to go to a different exit.

The cartels hire engineers to design the tunnels. They once broke a cartel boss out of jail by digging a tunnel all the way to the toilet in his cell!

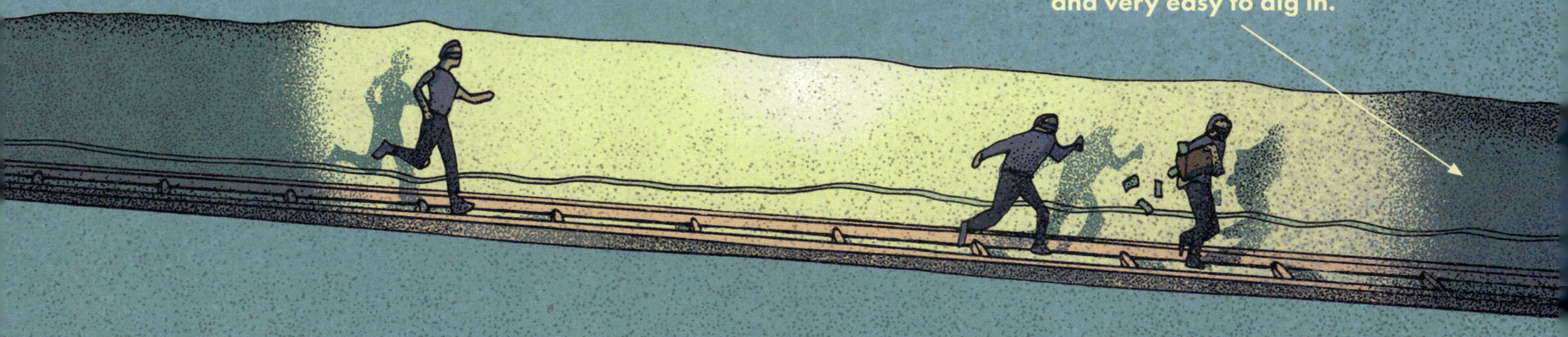

DRAMMEN SPIRAL

(Drammen, Norway, 1953–1961)

The people of Drammen needed a road to get to the top of the mountain, but they were worried about the impact it would have on the environment. The last thing they wanted was another ugly road on their beautiful mountain. Usually, mountain roads require lots of twists, bridges and tunnels. Can you guess what they came up with instead of this? A tunnel that goes up in a spiral inside the mountain!

This way, cars can reach the top of the mountain through a tunnel, and nothing spoils the view from outside except for the entrance and the exit.

LIGHTING

The tunnel has a clever lighting system that changes color depending on the time of the day. It can even simulate the aurora borealis!

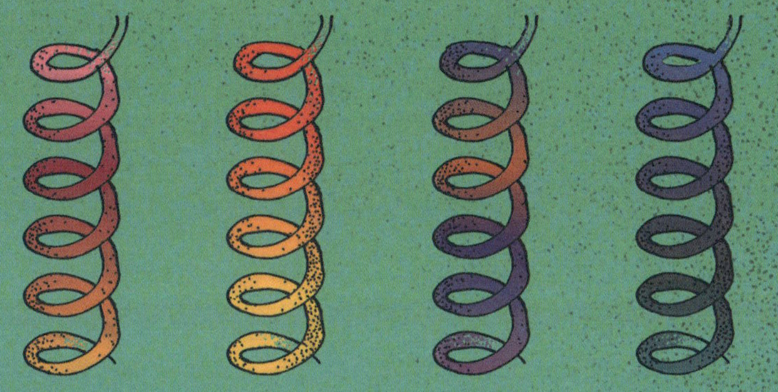

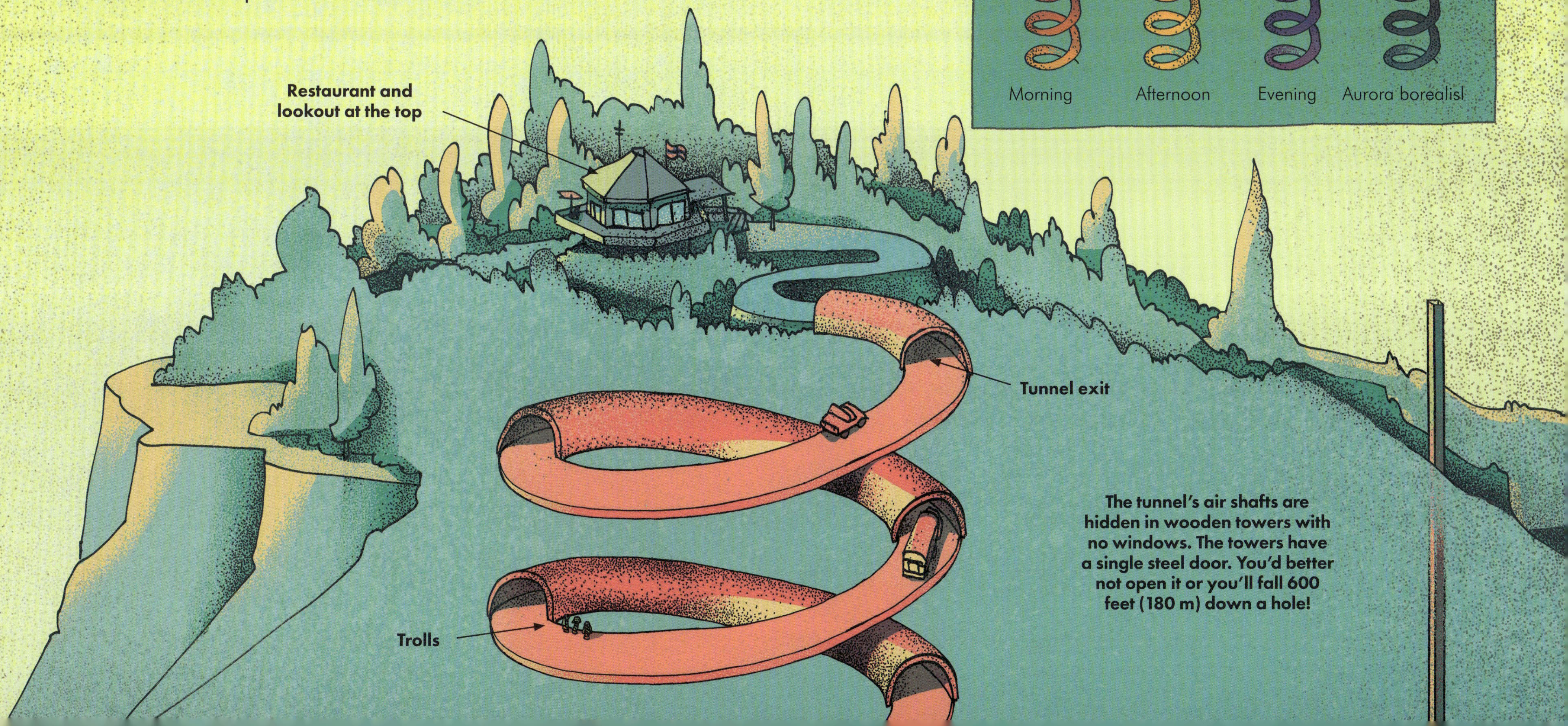

NOTHING GOES TO WASTE

They crushed the rocks they dug up and used them to form the city port.

IT GOES ROUND AND ROUND

The helix-shaped tunnel is one mile (1.6 km) long and made of six ascending rings. Construction began in 1953, and the tunnel was opened to the public by King Olav V in 1961.

THE BIG BLUE PIPE

The LHC is emptier than even the vacuum of outer space. This is so particles don't collide with gas molecules, which would ruin the experiments.

There are seven sensors around the particle beams, which collect important scientific data. The Large Hadron Collider generates some 20 petabytes of data every year. To put that in perspective, a high-definition movie of your entire life would take only half a petabyte!

The LHC holds another record: it is the world's biggest fridge. Tons of liquid helium are needed to keep its magnets at around -456°F (-271°C).

The collider uses as much energy as a third of the entire city of Geneva.

LHC, THE LARGE HADRON COLLIDER

(France–Switzerland border, 1989–2001)

A hadron collider uses awesome technology to make particles collide with each other at almost the speed of light. This way we can study these particles and learn a lot about the universe. Sound complicated? Well, it definitely is!

Accelerating particles to such speeds requires a straight line so long that Earth isn't big enough for it. So, CERN (European Organization for Nuclear Research) came up with the idea to build a huge underground ring. It's so vast that if you look up close it's almost like a straight line!

The first ring, built in 1976, was called SPS. It was 4.3 miles (7 km) long, but by 1996 it was too small for the experiments the scientists wanted to perform. The modern ring is called LHC and it's 17 miles (27 km) long. It's the biggest machine ever built, but CERN is already working on building an even bigger one. It will be 60 miles (100 km) long and ten times more powerful!

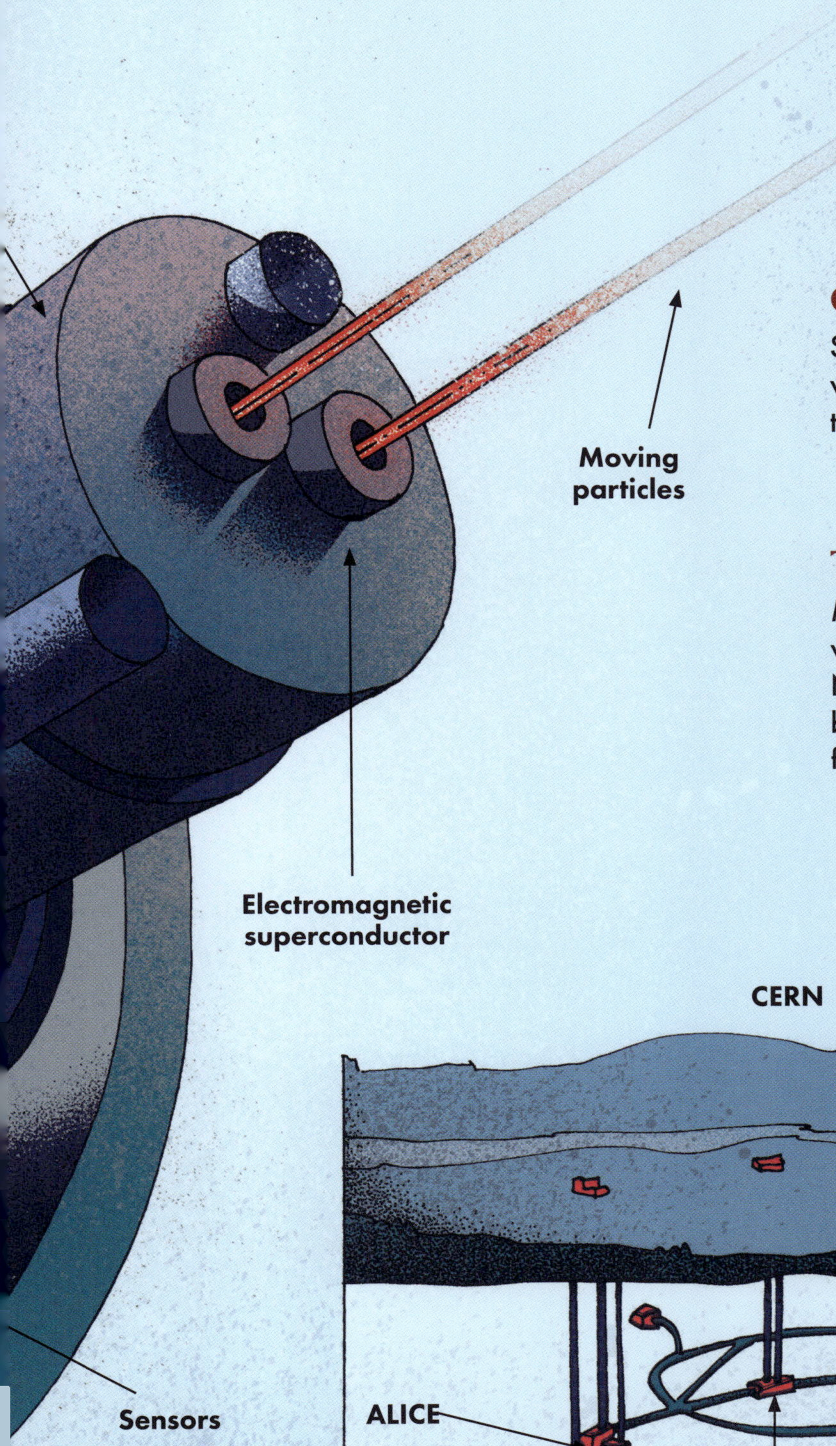

COMPUTER CONNECTION

Scientists needed to access research data from anywhere in the world, so in 1989 they designed a system that connected multiple devices. The internet was born!

THE END OF THE WORLD

Many people believed that a machine like the LHC would create a black hole and destroy the Earth. None of that happened, of course, and the LHC has been working for a decade without issues... except for a nosy weasel that got inside the tunnels!

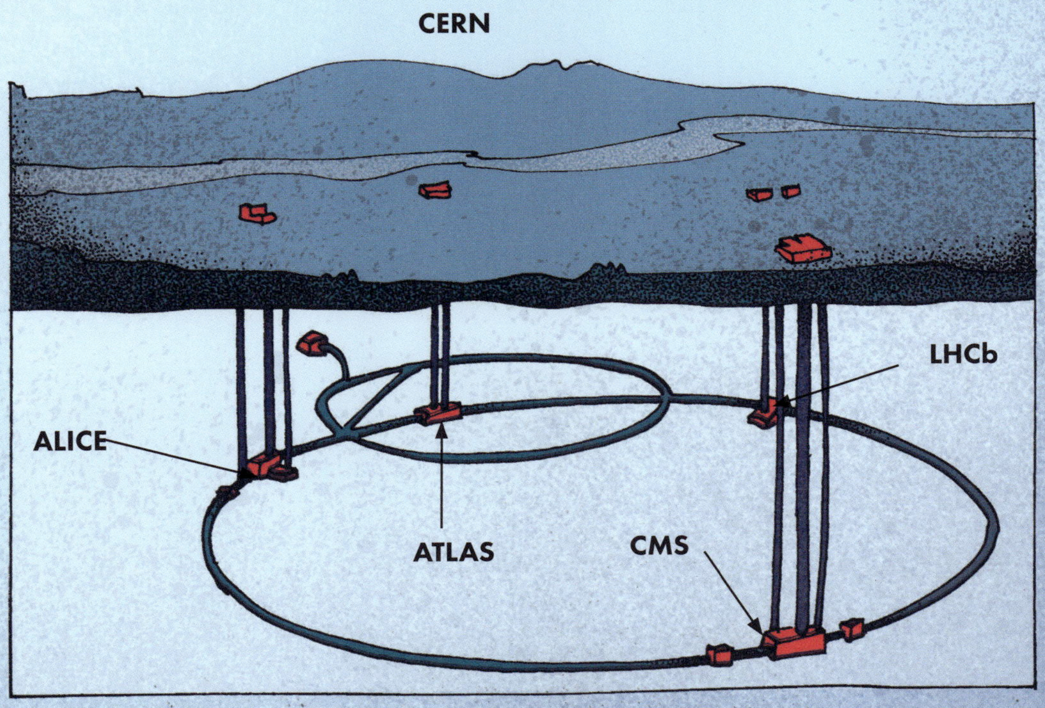

WASH YOUR HANDS AND NO TOUCHING!

It's super important to avoid contamination of the samples, so nobody is allowed to touch them once they're stored in boxes. Access to the facility is restricted, and most of the work is done remotely at the NordGen (Nordic Genetic Resource Center) headquarters.

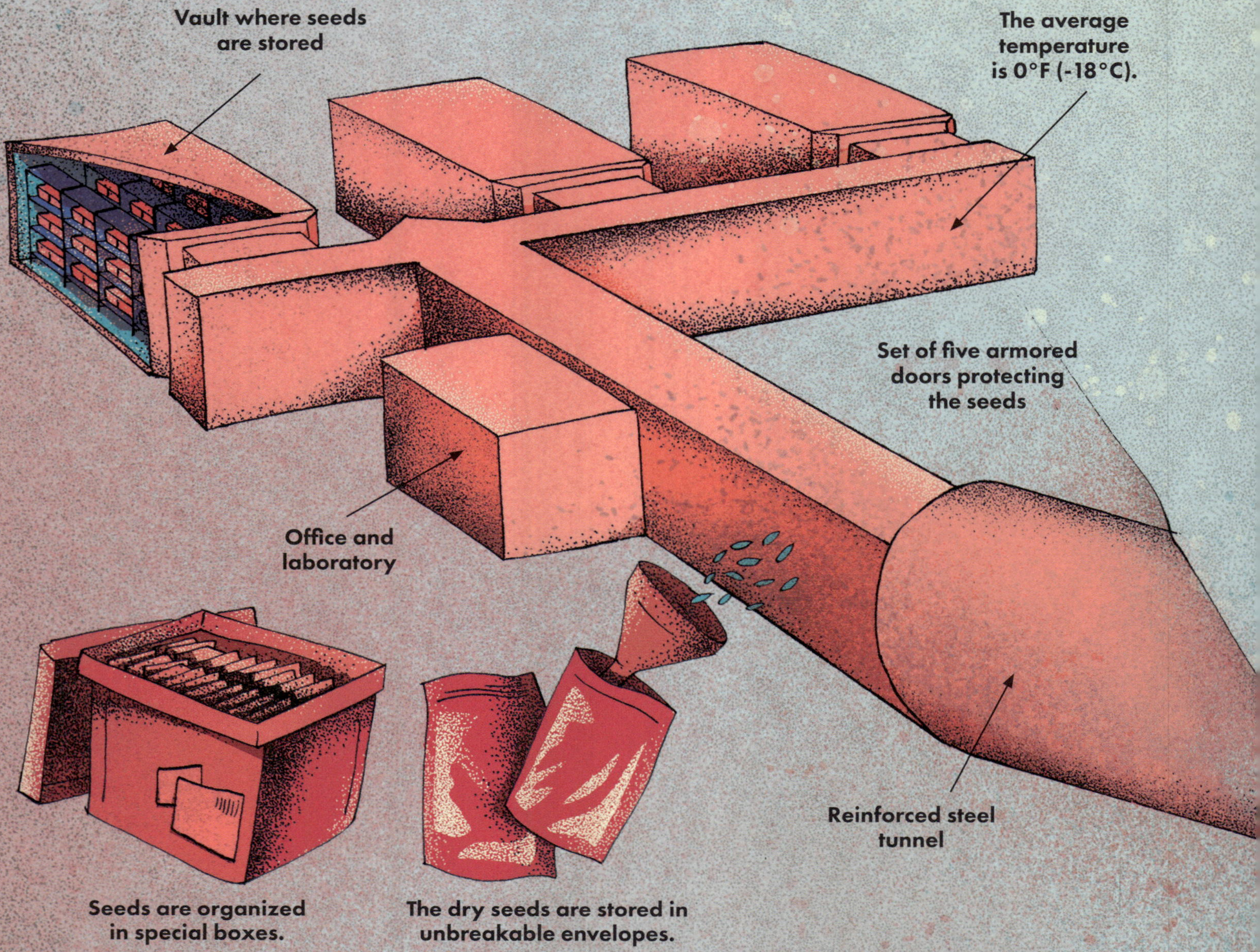

THE SVALBARD GLOBAL SEED VAULT

(Svalbard, Norway, 2006–2008)

There's a remote island in the Arctic Ocean, north of Norway, where it's so cold that snow never melts. There, you'll find a small building that looks like a comic book villain's secret lair. From the outside it just looks like a strange concrete dome on an icy island, but inside is where things get interesting. The building consists of three levels dug into the rocky terrain and kept at 0°F (-18°C). It's designed to resist volcanic eruptions, earthquakes, bombs and all sorts of disasters.

But what is so important that we need to keep it there? The answer: seeds. This is the world's biggest seed storage and its job is to preserve agricultural biodiversity in case of natural disasters. It's like a backup of a computer file: if something goes terribly wrong and a species of plant or crop is lost, we can use the contents of this vault to restore it.

Several plant species have been recovered after wars and floods thanks to this emergency backup.

The Svalbard Global Seed Vault has an area of 11,000 square feet (1000 square meters).

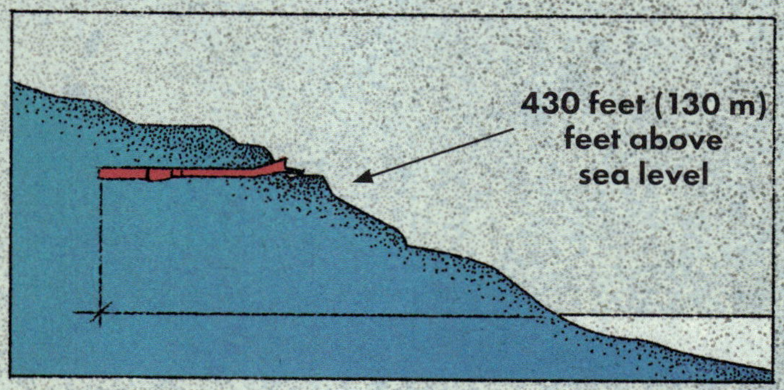

The vault holds more than one million different seeds. There are seven million crop plants in the world, and more than two million are unique species, so there are still plenty of seeds we need to add to the collection.

The Cherokee people sent a few samples of their Cherokee White Eagle Corn seed to be stored in the vault, since it's a sacred element in their culture.

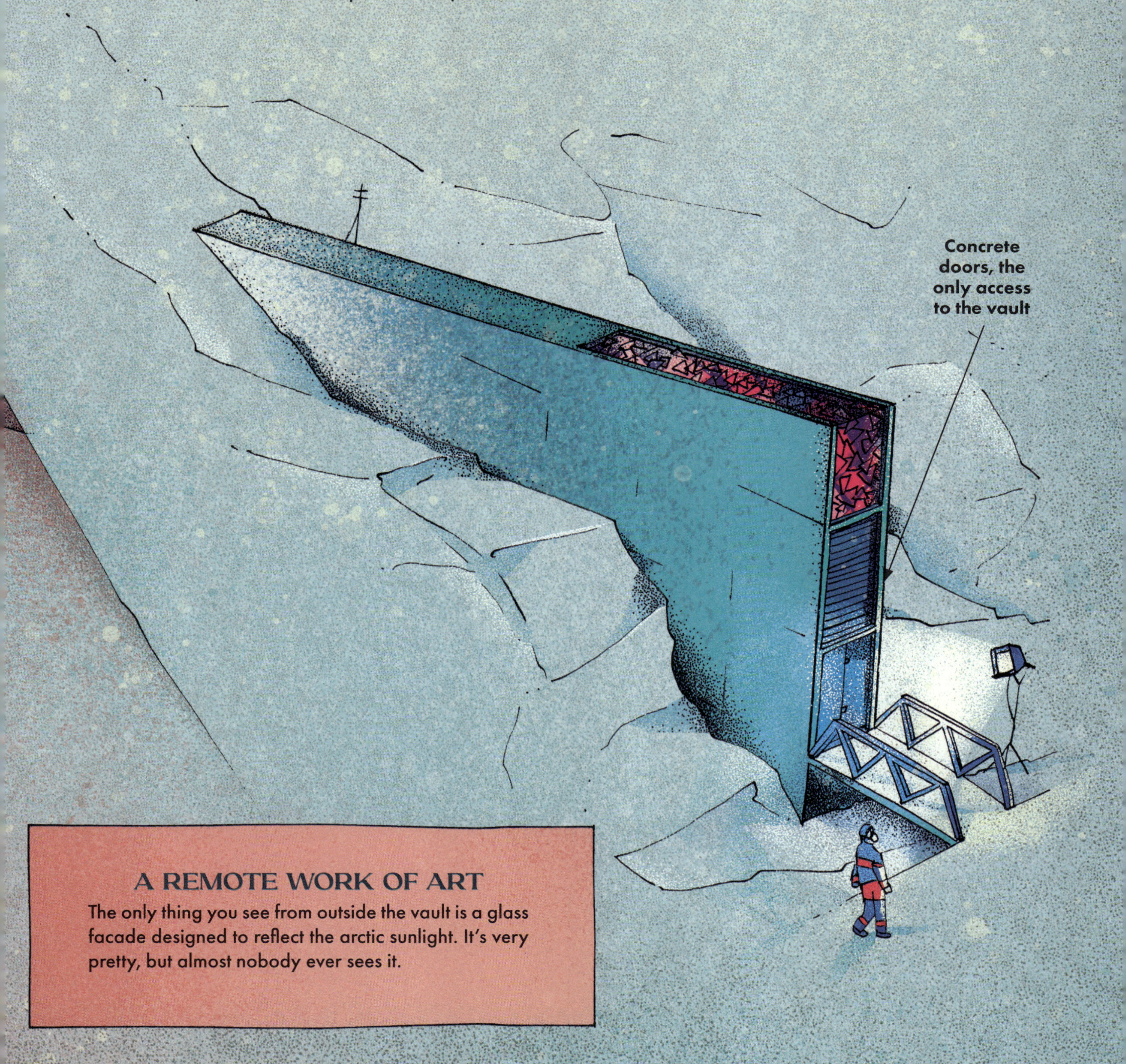

A REMOTE WORK OF ART

The only thing you see from outside the vault is a glass facade designed to reflect the arctic sunlight. It's very pretty, but almost nobody ever sees it.

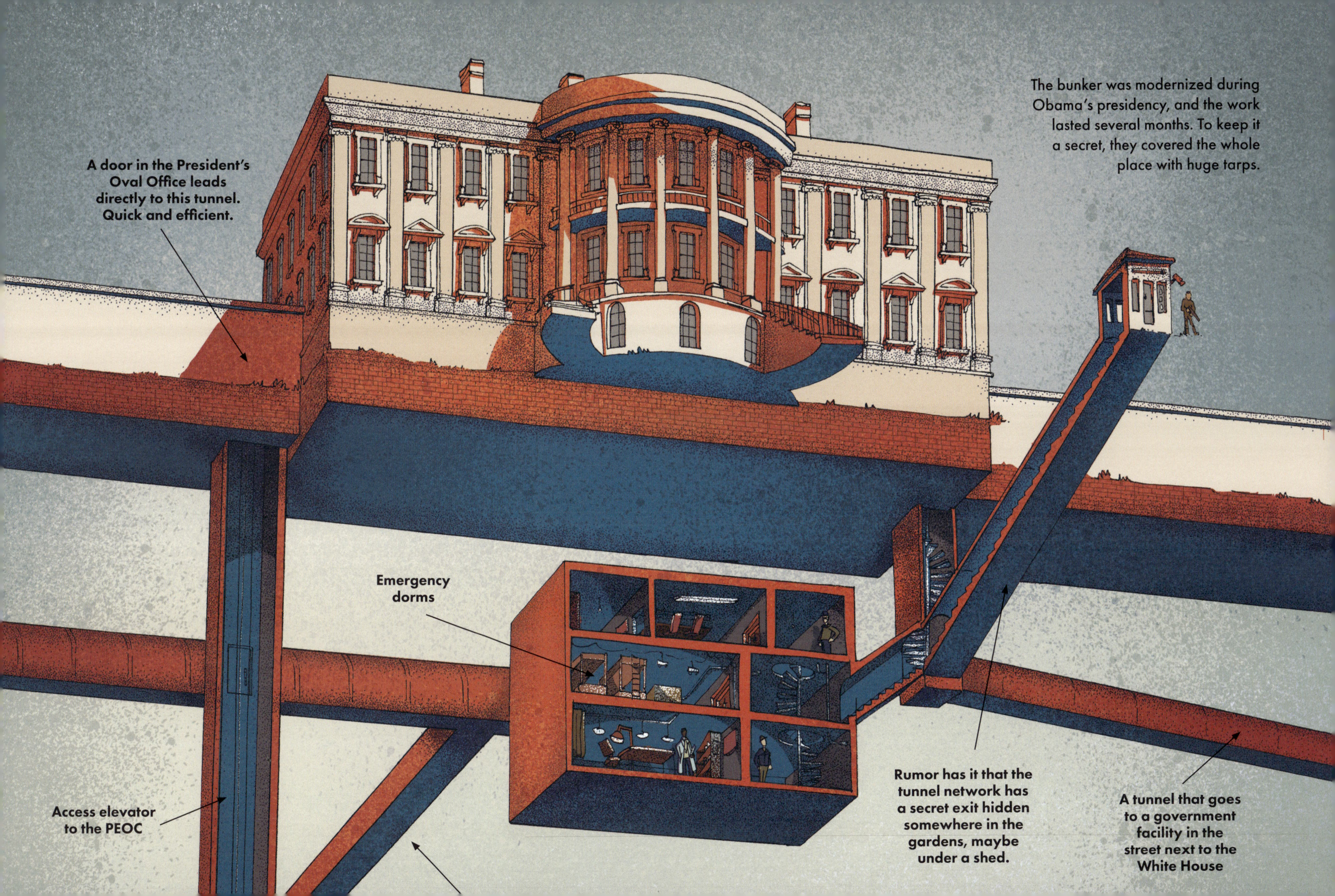
A door in the President's Oval Office leads directly to this tunnel. Quick and efficient.
The bunker was modernized during Obama's presidency, and the work lasted several months. To keep it a secret, they covered the whole place with huge tarps.
Emergency dorms
Access elevator to the PEOC
Rumor has it that the tunnel network has a secret exit hidden somewhere in the gardens, maybe under a shed.
A tunnel that goes to a government facility in the street next to the White House

This tunnel leads to a building several blocks away from the White House. The building looks like any other, but it is under strict surveillance.

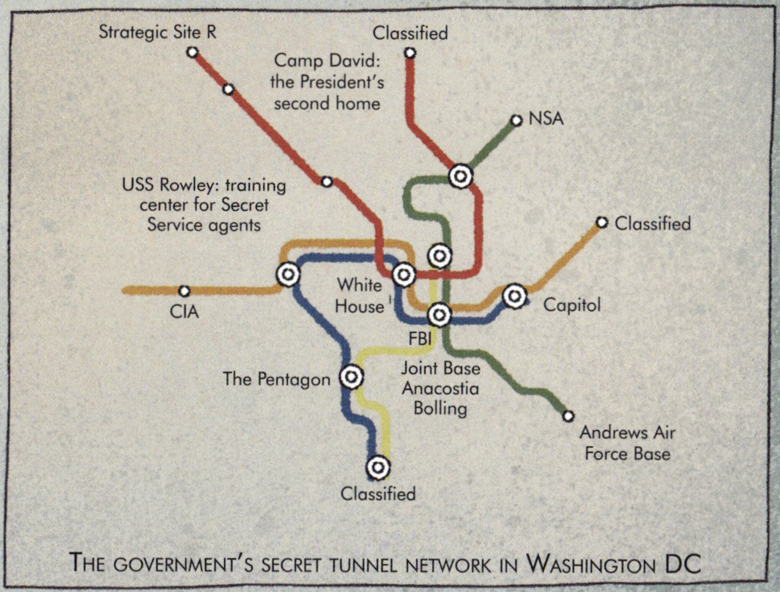

THE GOVERNMENT'S SECRET TUNNEL NETWORK IN WASHINGTON DC

Communication with the outside world is possible from the ops room.

THE WHITE HOUSE BUNKER

(Washington DC, the USA, 1941)

The White House is the US President's official home and workspace. It's where some of the most important decisions in the whole world are made, so it's no wonder it has an emergency bunker.

The White House was built in 1800, long before flying bombers were a thing. But after the attack on Pearl Harbor during the Second World War, President Roosevelt realized that the biggest threat came from the skies. Nothing could touch the White House on land, but what if the enemy just dropped bombs on it? With this in mind, the government decided to build a network of tunnels and rooms under the White House. To do this, they had to tear down the whole place, leaving only the front of the building standing as they worked on the underground bunker. Once that was done, they rebuilt and modernized the interior.

The bunker consists of a tunnel network that lets people move around secretly, and some of the tunnels have secret evacuation exits. There are also facilities where people could survive for a long time, like kitchens, dorms, storehouses, and even a hospital! The PEOC, or Presidential Emergency Operations Center, is the most important part. This room is equipped with advanced technology that would allow the president to work from there. It's so deep underground that if a nuclear bomb ever hit the surface, the people in the bunker wouldn't even notice!

PEOC, THE SAFEST PLACE IN THE USA

This is the ops room where members of the US government sheltered during the 9/11 attacks.

WHAT'S IN THE TUNNEL?

Actually, we have three tunnels here. One for each passenger line, and one in the middle for maintenance and emergency evacuations. They are connected every 1230 feet (375 m).

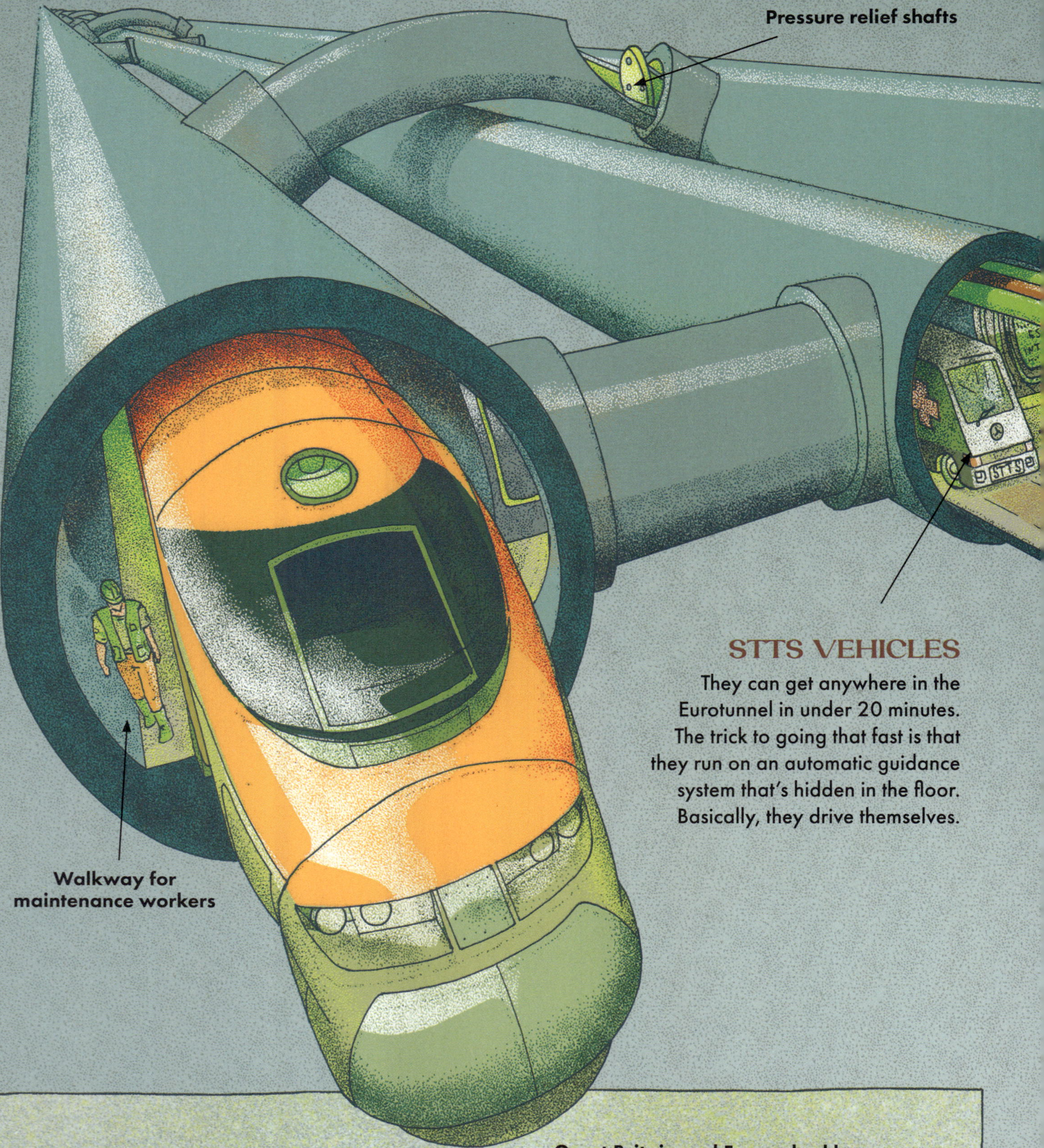

STTS VEHICLES

They can get anywhere in the Eurotunnel in under 20 minutes. The trick to going that fast is that they run on an automatic guidance system that's hidden in the floor. Basically, they drive themselves.

DIGGING THE GROUND

Building the Eurotunnel was a huge engineering challenge. The digging machines were so big they even had their own dining room for the workers!

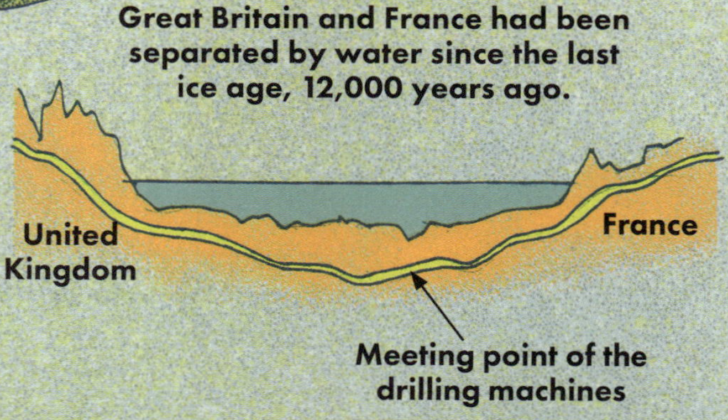

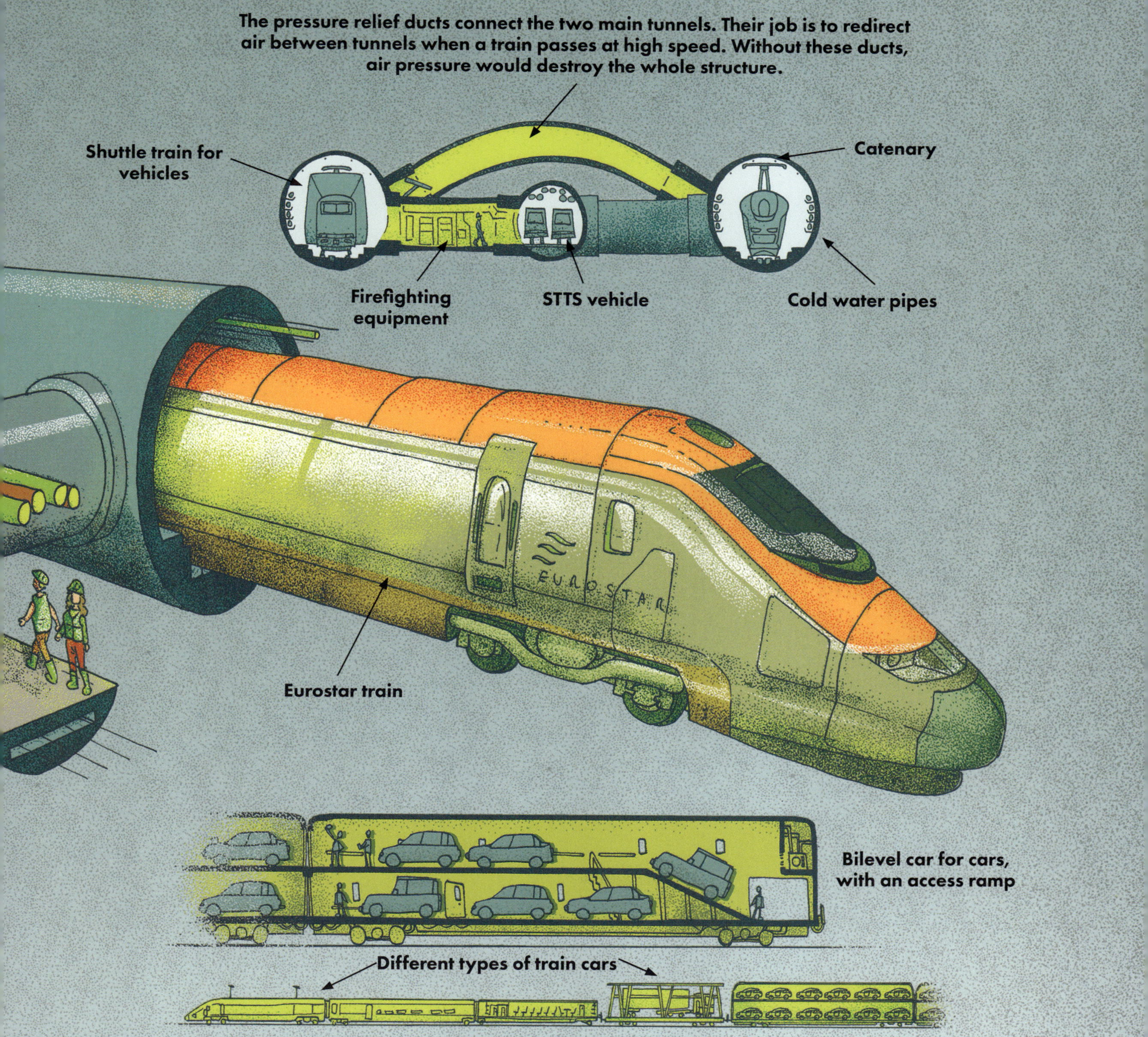

THE CHANNEL TUNNEL

(English Channel, between France and the United Kingdom, 1988–1994)

The only thing that separates the British Isles from mainland Europe is a 21-mile (34-km at its narrowest point) strip of water called the English Channel. For centuries, ships have been sailing between France and the UK here, moving people and goods. But throughout the years, people always had an idea that seemed impossible: what if we built a tunnel that linked both countries?

Many people believed this was a great idea. Napoleon himself greenlit a project to build a tunnel in 1882, but that wasn't really realistic until a century later. Even with the technology available in 1988, digging a 31-mile (50 km) tunnel wasn't easy at all. Gigantic tunnel boring machines dug into each coast and drilled through hard rock until the two tunnels met more than 300 feet (100 m) under the sea. These machines didn't just drill the ground; they also left each section of the tunnel finished behind them as they moved forward.

Construction lasted seven years. Finally, the Channel Tunnel opened in 1994, making it possible to go from France to the UK by train.

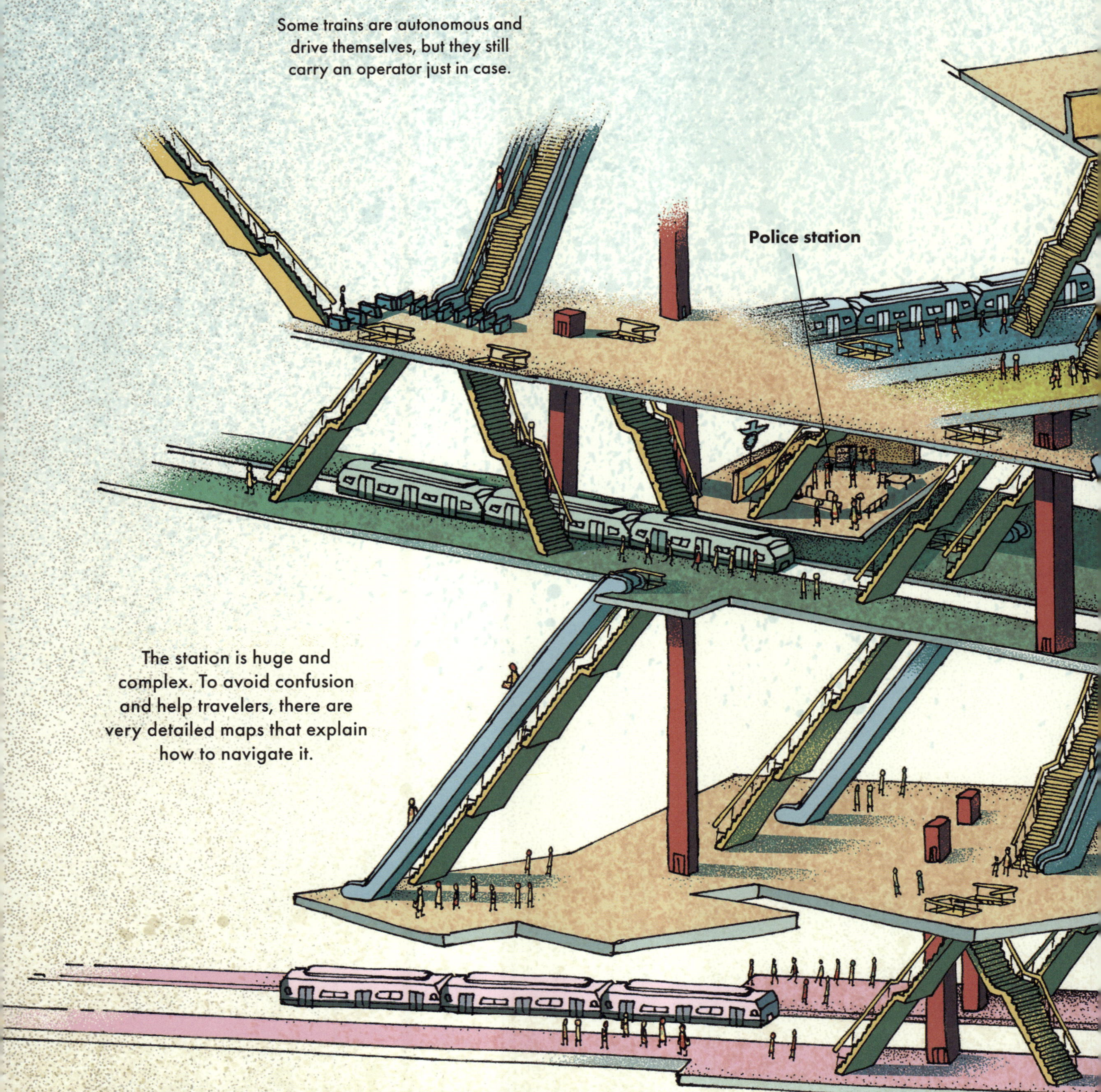

THE SEOUL SUBWAY

(Seoul, South Korea, 1971–1974)

By the time the Seoul Subway started moving passengers, the London Underground was almost 100 years old. Although it's rather new, it's already the world's biggest subway network. It connects each district in the city, and it also goes to other cities and provinces. More than seven million passengers travel on its 200 miles (320 km) of subway lines each day.

There are 293 stations in total! Usually, the trains travel at just 19 mph (30 kph). Seoul citizens on average spend about two hours commuting to and from work every day, so the network is being upgraded to allow trains to travel at 112 mph (180 kph).

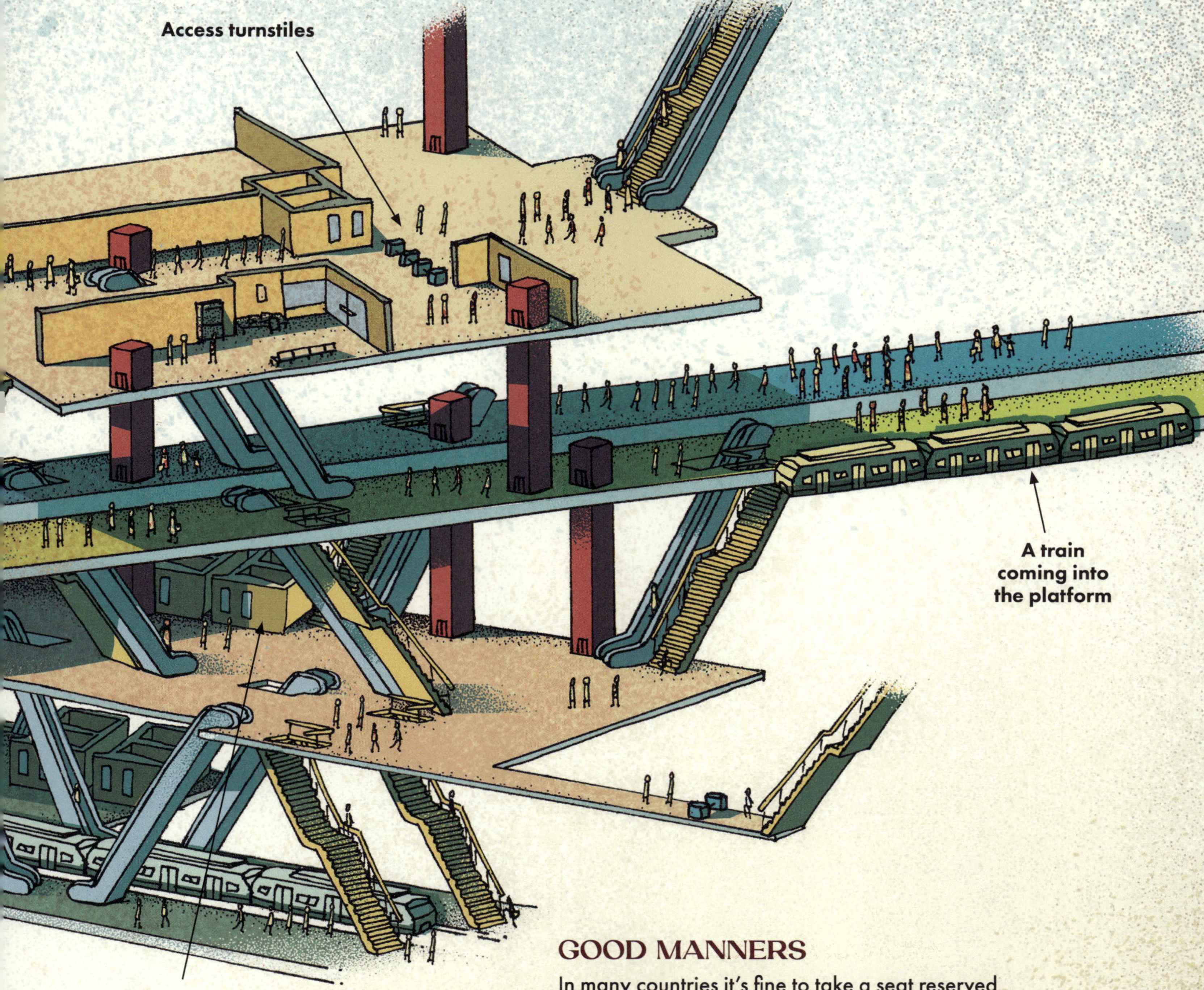

GOOD MANNERS

In many countries it's fine to take a seat reserved for elderly or disabled people if they're not needed, but that's frowned upon in Korea.

Despite the huge amounts of people that use it, the Seoul Subway is the cleanest in the world. Don't even think about littering!

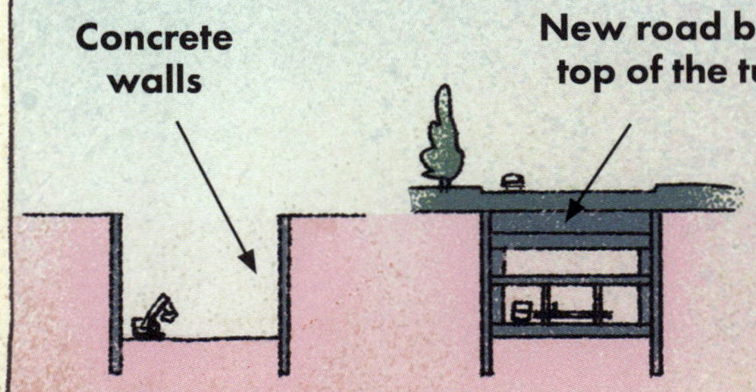

DIGGING THE TUNNEL

Work on the first section of the tunnel started in 1971 using the cut-and-cover method. First, they dug a trench on the street. Then, they built the tunnel. Finally, they covered it and rebuilt the street on top of it. It may sound complicated, but this was the cheapest way to build a subway.

THE BIG DIG

(Boston, the USA, 1991–2007)

Americans really love their highways.

Fast cars, endless landscapes and the feeling of total freedom: the country was founded before cars were even invented, but that didn't stop the US from building a network of thousands of miles of roads starting in the early 20th century.

The highways helped connect cities and move people and goods around, but they weren't free of problems: noise, pollution, and neighborhoods split in two by huge roads.

CITIES FOR THE PEOPLE!

Some parts of American cities were designed for cars from the start, with little consideration for people who might want to walk.

The city of Boston built a huge highway right through the downtown. Very useful for drivers, but terrible for urban life: it was loud, ugly, bad for the environment. Places that used to be a short walk from each other were now separated by busy roads.

Then, someone had an idea: why not move the highway underground and build parks, sidewalks and squares on the surface? The project was called the Big Dig.

It sounded like a great plan, but it was plagued by issues. Construction lasted almost 25 years and it was much more expensive than originally planned. Mistakes were made, politicians fought over it, and serious accidents happened. The whole project was so messy that, even after it was finished, people thought of the Big Dig as how not to do things.

Shipwrecks from the 19th century were found during the excavation process!

How do you dig while preventing the ground from collapsing? You use coolant tubes to freeze the ground!

YOU COULD DO BETTER

The Big Dig might have been a mess, but that doesn't mean it was a bad idea. There are places where it worked very well: in Seoul, in South Korea, a highway that ran over a river was replaced with a promenade complete with trees and water areas. And in Barcelona, in Spain, they buried a very busy avenue and built a huge park in its place.

Today, many cities are adopting this way of thinking. Do we really need cars to be everywhere in our daily lives? Wouldn't it be better to have more room for walking, cycling, or just sitting on a bench under some trees? It's not about getting rid of cars, but about finding a nice balance. Highways were great in their time, but the future of big cities could be much nicer if we start building for people first.

Nothing is wasted here. The water goes to a recycling plant so it can be reused.

DIZZY TOWN

If the unstable ground wasn't enough, Mexico City also gets a lot of earthquakes. That's why it sinks about 4 inches (10 cm) every year and many of its old buildings are leaning.

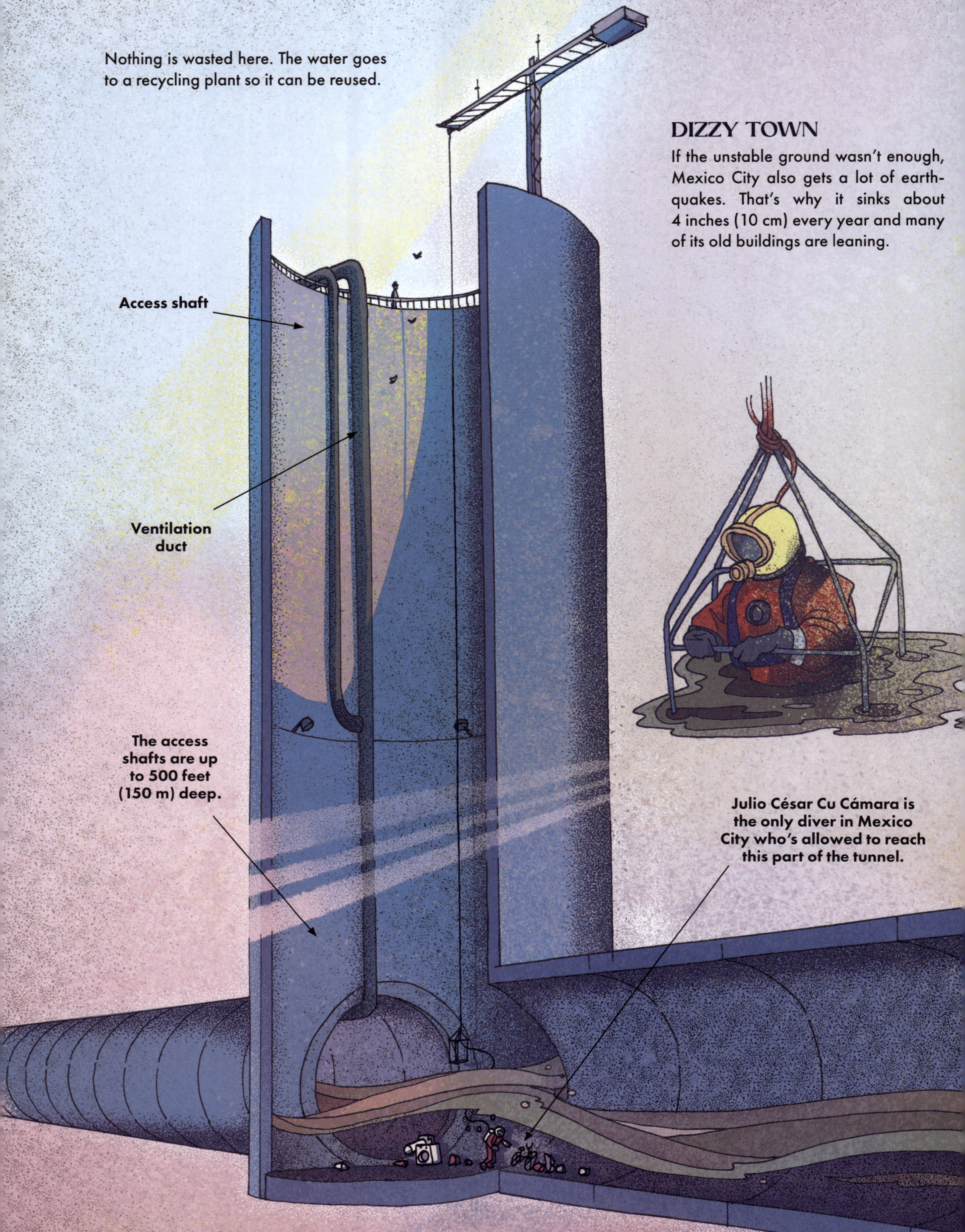

THE EASTERN DISCHARGE TUNNEL

(Mexico City, 2008–2019)

Mexico City is one of the biggest cities in the world, but also one of the most unstable. There used to be a lake here! Tenochtitlan, as the city was known in the 16th century, stood on six small lakes that grew and formed the bigger Lake Texcoco during the rainy season. When the Spanish arrived, they destroyed the city's water regulation system and had to build a new one.

As the city expanded, the lakes were dried up to create artificial islands connected by canals. Eventually, the city grew so big that it covered the whole lake. This means that during the rainy season, many rivers sprout up and a lot of water rushes in to fill the old lake. The problem is, since the lake isn't there anymore, the city is flooded instead!

To fix this, they built a network of deep drainage tunnels to move all that water away from the city. But there is a problem with this, too: the city sits on very soft soil, which causes the tunnels to deform and stop working. The Eastern Discharge Tunnel was opened in 2019, after an awesome tunneling machine spent 11 years digging 40 feet (13 m) of tunnels every day. This is one of the most important engineering marvels of this century. It's almost 40 miles (62 km) long, and 40,000 gallons of water can flow through it every second!

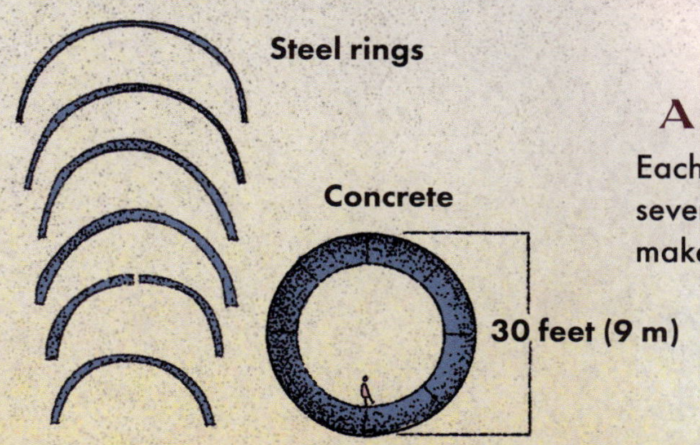

A HARD TUNNEL

Each section of the tunnel has seven reinforced structures that make it almost unbreakable.

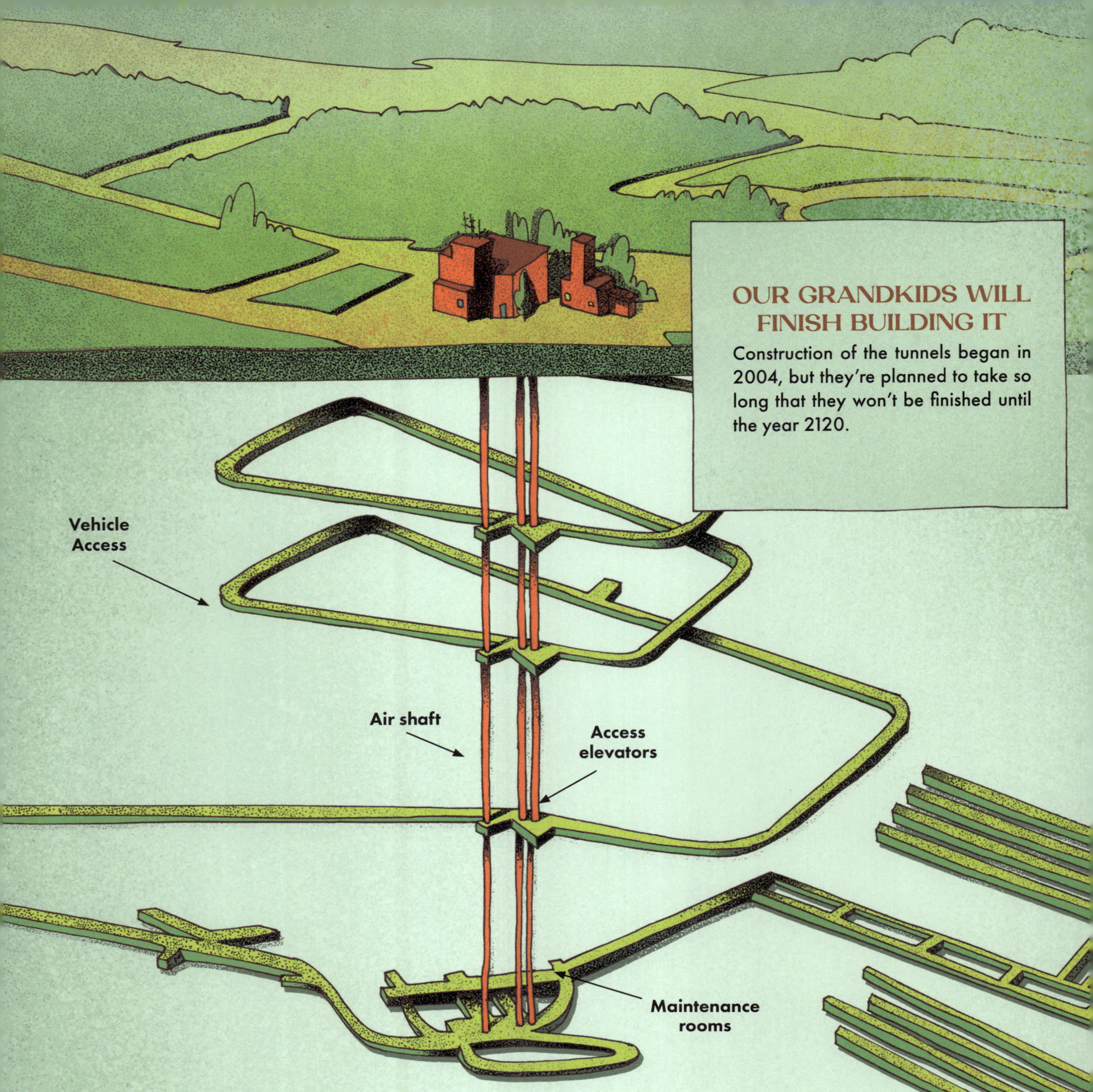

OUR GRANDKIDS WILL FINISH BUILDING IT

Construction of the tunnels began in 2004, but they're planned to take so long that they won't be finished until the year 2120.

DANGER, DO NOT TOUCH!

Scientists worry that, thousands of years from now, humans from the future might find this place and not know what it is. They will just see a bunch of strange copper boxes left behind by an ancient civilization. It would be very dangerous if they opened them!

This sign will go on the entrance to the tunnels, as a warning.

THE ONKALO NUCLEAR WASTE REPOSITORY

(Eurajoki, Finland, 2004)

Usually, we burn fuels like gas or coal to generate electricity. But this produces a lot of pollution and contributes to global warming, so we've been looking for cleaner ways to obtain energy. Those include solar, wind and tidal power. When scientists discovered nuclear energy, they thought they'd found the holy grail: they found that nuclear reactions release a lot of energy. This energy was pretty cheap, since they could get plenty of power for a long time from just a little bit of radioactive fuel. Plus, it seemed that the only waste it created was harmless water vapor. Does that sound too good to be true? Well, about that...

One of the big problems with nuclear power is that it can be very toxic. Nuclear powerplants use radioactive fuel that could kill a person in a few seconds, even if they are far away, and it can damage the environment for hundreds of years. If that's not enough, nuclear fuel takes millions of years to stop being so dangerous. Nuclear residue buried during the dinosaur age would still be a problem for us today. Nuclear power plants keep radiation in check, held back by multiple layers of concrete, lead and water. But what happens when we have to dispose of all the nuclear waste?

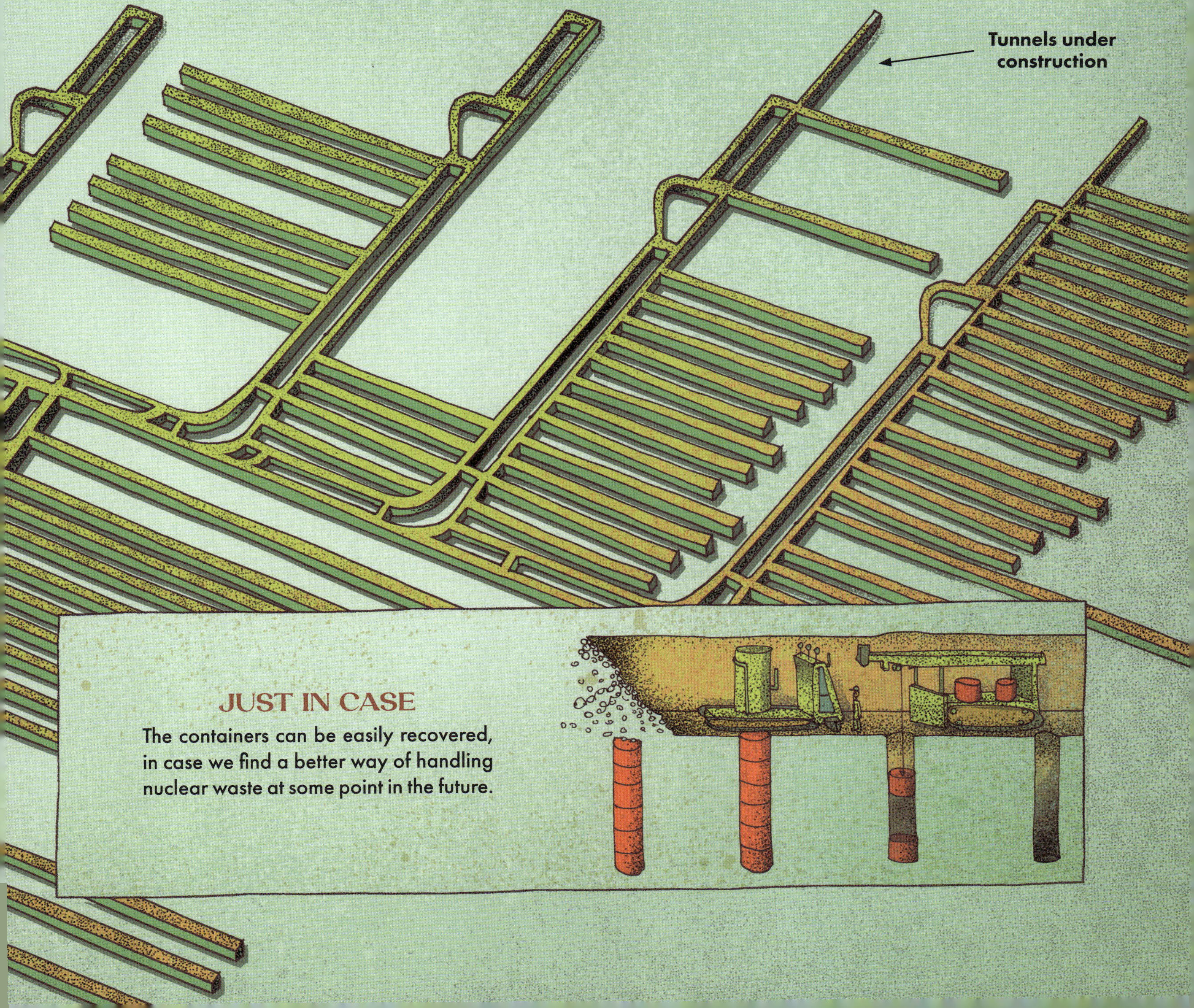

JUST IN CASE

The containers can be easily recovered, in case we find a better way of handling nuclear waste at some point in the future.

WATCH YOUR HEAD

The ceiling is so low that many modern cars don't fit in it. Some people started asking for a new tunnel to be built, but it's best to let things stay natural with minimal intervention. We don't want to spoil the environment!

TUNNEL LOG

(California, USA, 1957)

Many tunnels are huge and amazing constructions that require complex engineering and hundreds of workers. But sometimes, you just need a little hole to cross a small distance. One day in 1937, rangers at the Sequoia National Park in California were doing their rounds in the woods when they found something unusual on the road: a massive fallen sequoia was blocking the road!

This incident had natural causes. Sequoias live very long, and this one was so old that its roots couldn't support the weight of the tree anymore. This problem had a simple solution. Instead of moving the whole tree, they just cut a hole in it big enough for a car to drive through. The hole is 8 feet (2.4 m) tall and 17 feet (5.2 m) wide, and nowadays it's a popular landmark. So many tourists stop here to take selfies in the tunnel that they cause traffic jams!

MARTIAN HABITATS

Houses on Mars will be quite cozy. AI SpaceFactory's Marsha habitat design is a four-story building shaped like an egg with double walls to keep you warm and safe, and a spiral staircase inside.

BRING YOUR COAT

Temperatures along the Martian equator reach 95°F (35°C), but they can also get as low as -130°F (-89°C).

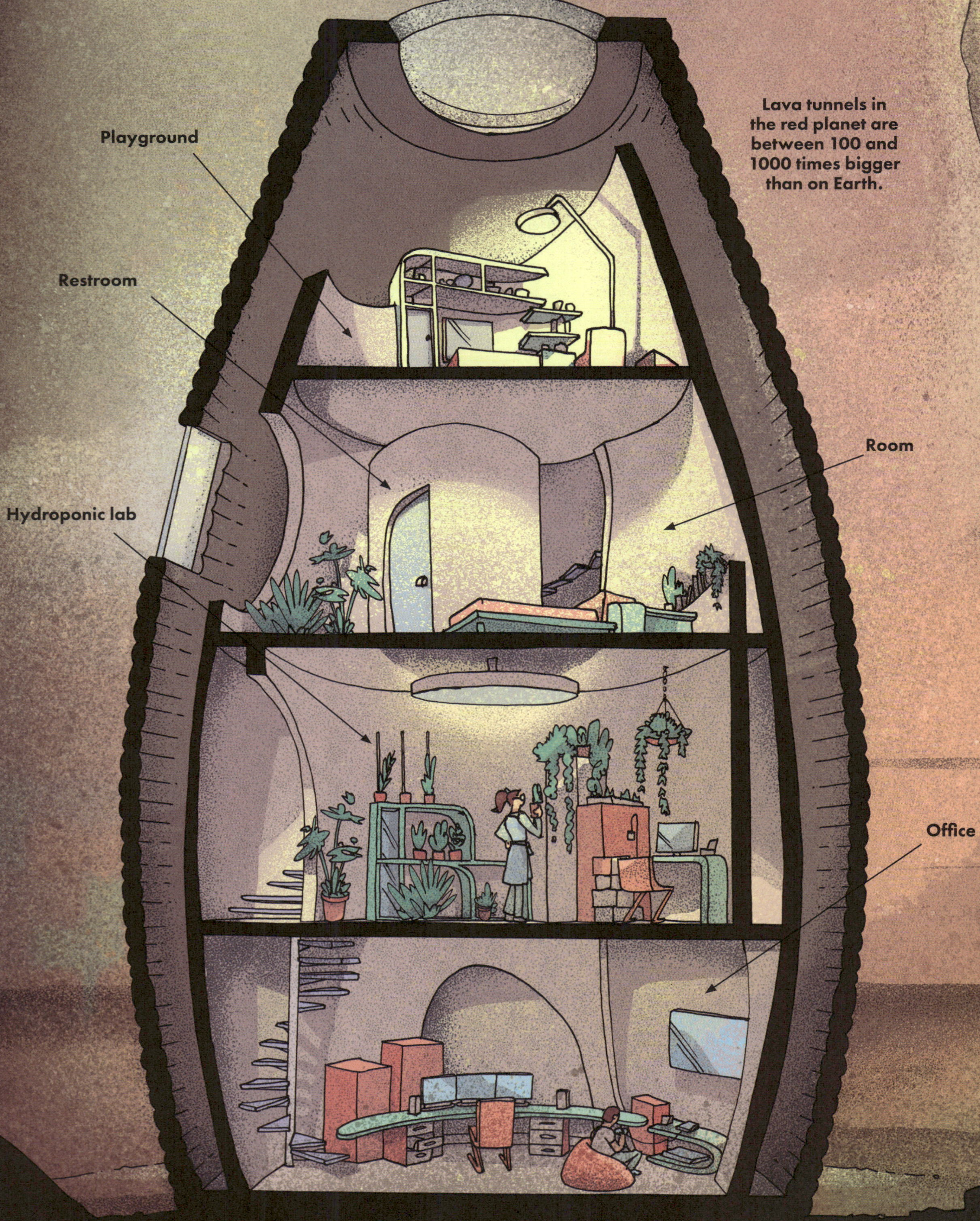

Lava tunnels in the red planet are between 100 and 1000 times bigger than on Earth.

LIFE ON MARS

If you've ever been in a natural cave, you know they're cold, dark and not very comfy. Nobody would want to live in such a place, right? Well, a group of scientists wants to do exactly that... but on Mars!

Natural caves on Mars are gigantic. You could fit all of Central Park in some of them, and we believe there are caves bigger than Manhattan there. These caves were formed millions of years ago due to lava currents flowing to the surface. When the lava cooled, it left behind huge empty tunnels. Scientists believe these natural caves could protect humans from Martian hazards such as ultraviolet rays, sandstorms and space radiation.

Everything is planned out. First, we'll plant crops on Martian soil under huge domes, using water extracted from underground frozen lakes. Then, by mixing plant compounds with sand mined from the tunnels, we'll make cement. And then, a huge 3D printer will fabricate a bunch of habitats for the colony.

Would you move to Mars? The plan is for more than a hundred people to live there, but don't get too excited about having your own house on another planet: we haven't even sent probes to explore the tunnels yet.

GLOSSARY

ADOBE Brick made of sun-dried mud and hay

AQUEDUCT Artificial channel made to move large amounts of water

ARCHAEOLOGIST A person who researches civilizations by studying the fossils, buildings, materials, documents and human remains they leave behind

ASCENDING Going up

ATOM The smallest unit of an element (such as oxygen or iron)

AURORA BOREALIS Natural phenomenon of colorful, shifting lights that can be seen near the North Pole

BUNKER Underground shelter made of reinforced concrete

CAMOUFLAGE To hide something by making it look like the nearby terrain

CEMENT Powder that hardens when you mix it with water

CLAY Fine earth mixed with water to make mud

COLLAPSE Destruction of a structure caused by a force

CONCRETE Mix of gravel, lime, cement, sand and water. We call it *reinforced concrete* when it has metal bars inside that make it even stronger.

DEMOLITION Controlled destruction of something using explosives

DITCH Hole in the ground

DOME Arch-shaped ceiling

ENGINEER A person who uses science to design all sorts of things, from buildings and irrigation systems to anti-theft alarms

FOGOU Cornish word that means *cave*

GROTTO Cave

HYDROPONICS A method of farming used to grow vegetables in a lab

ICE AGE A long period of extreme cold and icy weather

LACUSTRINE Related to a lake

LAVA Extremely hot molten rock that comes out of a volcano

MOLECULE A group of atoms

NICHE Hole on a wall where people put statues and other things

PARTICLE A very tiny piece of a material

PINNACLE Building decoration shaped like a spiky cone

PYRITE Sulfur and iron mineral with a metallic yellow color that looks like gold

QUARRY Place where rock and stone are excavated

RADIOACTIVITY Something that emits energy through radiation. Radioactive materials can be dangerous for people and the environment, but they are also useful for making energy.

RAIL Metal piece that a vehicle can slide on

RUDIMENTARY Basic, simple, primitive

SEQUOIA Huge and long-lived trees that are native to some parts of the United States

SIEGE Military operation where an army surrounds the enemy and traps them in a fortified place. This forces the enemy to surrender when they run out of food and water.

SKYLIGHT Hole in the ceiling that brings in light and air from outside

SUBTERRANEAN Underground

TUNNEL A man-made underground path that links two places and has many uses

TUNNEL BORING MACHINE A huge machine used to drill soil and build tunnels

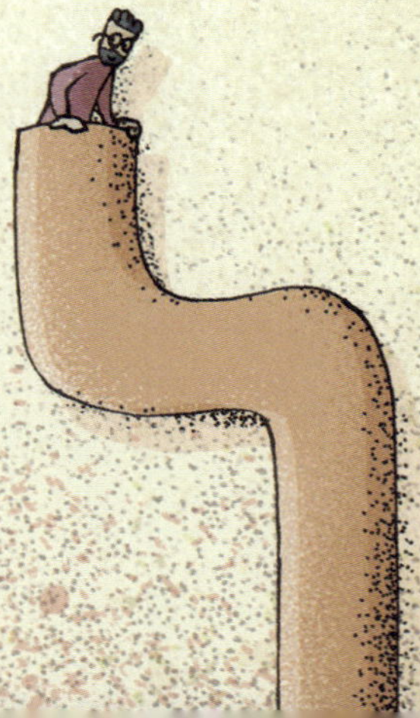